LOVE LOVES A PORNOGRAPHER

(or PLEASE AS YOU PLEASE)

Jeff Goode

BROADWAY PLAY PUBLISHING INC
New York
www.broadwayplaypublishing.com
info@broadwayplaypublishing.com

LOVE LOVES A PORNOGRAPHER
© Copyright 2008 by Jeff Goode

Cover image by Lee Moyer
1st printing: May 2008
I S B N: 978-0-88145-385-0
Book design: Marie Donovan
Word processing: Microsoft Word
Typographic controls: Ventura Publisher
Typeface: Palatino
Printed and bound in the U S A

LOVE LOVES A PORNOGRAPHER was presented as a workshop reading in the hotINK International Festival of Play Readings on 28 January 2007 at the Tisch School of Arts Department of Drama (The Classical Studio), Daniel Spector, Curator. The cast and creative contributor were:

FENNIMORE .... Larry Petersen
MILES MONGER .... Greg Jackson
MILLICENT MONGER .... Erin Quinn Purcell
LADY LOVEWORTHY .... Rosemary Quinn
LORD LOVEWORTHY ..... Timothy McCown Reynolds
EMILY LOVEWORTHY .... Kristen Sieh
EARL .... Steven Stout

Director .... Jeremy Dobrish

The world premiere production of LOVE LOVES A PORNOGRAPHER opened 17 November 2007 at [Inside] the Ford Theater in Los Angeles, a production of the Circle X Theater Company (produced by Tim Wright and Jillian Armenante, associate produced by Jennifer A Skinner). The cast and creative contributors were:

FENNIMORE ....Weston Nathanson
MILES MONGER ....Jim Anzide
MILLICENT MONGER .... Johannna McKay
LADY LOVEWORTHY ....Gillian Doyle
LORD LOVEWORTHY ....William Salyers
EMILY LOVEWORTHY ....Kathleen Rose Perkins
EARL ....Matt Ford

Understudies: Rebecca Avery, Alice Dodd, David Fruechting, John Lovick, Lily Rains, Doug Sutherland, Tim Wright

Director ....Jillian Armenante
Scenic design .... Gary Smoot
Lighting design ....Karl Gajdusek
Costume design .... Paul Spadone
Sound design ....Jillian Armenante
Prop design .... Ali Hisserich
Stage managed ....Mel Stone
Assistant directed .... Abigail Marateck
Assistant stage managed .... Kathleen Ressegger
Scenic artist ....Sharon Mayerchak
Master carpenter .... Chris Goodson
Board operator ....Rich Lehmann
Postcard/program design ....Kevin Fabian

Publicist . . . . Virginia Schneider
Photographer . . . . Benno Sebastian
House manager . . . . Paul Tigue

DRAMATIS PERSONAE

FENNIMORE, *a butler*
MILES MONGER, *a literary critic*
MILLICENT MONGER, *his wife, an avid reader*
SIR CYRIL LOVEWORTHY, *an acclaimed novelist*
LADY LILLIAN, *his wife, a diarist*
MISS EMILY LOVEWORTHY, *their daughter*
EARL KANT, *her fiancé*

To...

Patricia Decker

(without whom this play would be, hamster shavings)

and the Tisch School of Arts'
hotINK International Festival of Play Readings

Catherine Coray, Festival Director
Bev Mitchell, Producer
Marla Shaffer, Production Manager
Chantel Bilodeau, Literary Manager

And for lending their talent and encouragement to this
piece from the very beginning:

Eve Armstrong
Michele Begley
Bridget Ann White
Wayne Yeager

Thank you.

ACT ONE
Lord Loveworthy's Wager

(Scene: The Parlour of Loveworthy Manor.)

*(*FENNIMORE *the butler enters, clears his throat.)*

FENNIMORE: Ahem...The Reverend and Mrs Miles and Millicent Monger!

*(*MILES MONGER *enters, as if to thunderous applause, followed by his wife* MILLICENT, *quietly engrossed in a book.*

MILES: Good afternoon, your Lordship, what an unexpected pleasure it is to finally...and so graciously...be invited into...

(But the room is empty.)

MILES: Fennimore?

FENNIMORE: Yes, sir?

MILES: This room is unoccupied.

FENNIMORE: On the contrary, sir. You are in it.

MILES: But Lord Loveworthy and Lady Lillian are not.

FENNIMORE: That is a keen observation, sir

MILES: Why, then, did you bother to introduce us?

FENNIMORE: You asked to be introduced, sir.

MILLICENT: *(looking up from her book)* You did ask, Miles.

FENNIMORE: Rather insisted on it, as I recall.

MILLICENT: Quite prickly about it, in fact, weren't you, dear?

FENNIMORE: You seemed convinced of the need for a formal introduction, sir. And when a guest is mistaken, one prefers to err on the side of hospitality.

MILES: An error the Loveworthys have not condescended to commit.

MILLICENT: Perhaps they are unavoidably detained. Will Lady Lillian and Sir Cyril be joining us shortly, Fennimore?

FENNIMORE: I don't see as that's possible.

MILES: Are they not even on the premises?

FENNIMORE: Certainly they are. But it is a very large house. I doubt they are as yet aware of your arrival.

MILES: Can no one make them aware of it?

FENNIMORE: If you like, sir, but it's better if I do it.

(MILES *glowers*.)

MILLICENT: We would appreciate that, Fennimore, thank you.

(FENNIMORE *exits*.)

MILES: Well, here's a fine welcome!

MILLICENT: We must be the first to arrive.

MILES: That goes without saying, as we are the only ones here. And we are like to be the last to arrive, as well, as we are the only ones invited. It is to be you and I and the Loveworthys for tea this afternoon.

MILLICENT: Just the four of us? Won't that be lovely!

MILES: Indeed, it won't be lovely, if the Loveworthys do not deign to grace us with their attendance. What sort of host extends an invitation of a social engagement,

only to leave his guests entirely to their own diversion?
It is unconscionable.

MILLICENT: Must you always be so critical?

MILES: Yes, in fact, I must, my dear. I am, after all,
a critic. And no less a one than the chief literary critic
for the *Times* of London, the foremost periodical in Her
Majesty's kingdom. Therefore, it would be a betrayal
not only of my personal circumstances, but of the very
integrity of our national press, for me to be anything
less than acutely critical of all things at all times and in
all places. And it offends me, both as a journalist, and
as your husband, that you would have me abandon the
very characteristic which has defined both my life and
my livelihood for as long as we two have been married.

MILLICENT: You are right, of course. As always. But it's
hardly a wonder we are not invited to more garden
parties.

MILES: Yes, I'm sure I am entirely to blame for our
societal estrangement, as no one has ever been
ostracized for being an opinionless mop.

MILLICENT: Very well, I apologize. But there's no
need to be cruel. You know how it brings me to tears.
(Sobbing) Oh! There I go.

MILES: Well, compose yourself immediately. The
Loveworthys may be upon us at any moment.

(FENNIMORE enters, clears his throat.)

FENNIMORE: Ahem... The Lady Lillian Loveworthy!
Mistress of the Manor, and Lady of the House.
(Thought you might like that, sir.)

MILLICENT: Oh! She mustn't see me like this.
Fennimore, is there a powder room about?

FENNIMORE: There's likely a ladies' loo lurking in the
lobby. Right this way, ma'am.

MILES: *(To* MILLICENT*)* Go on, then!

(MILLICENT *follows* FENNIMORE *out of the room.)*

(LADY LILLIAN *enters, cheerfully at first, until she sees* MILES*.)*

LADY LILLIAN: Good afternoon, welcome, and my humblest apologies! I have only just been informed that... *You.*

MILES: *(Bowing)* Lady Lillian.

LADY LILLIAN: What are you doing here?

MILES: I was invited.

LADY LILLIAN: *(Seething)* That was a very long time ago.

MILES: You mistake my meaning.

LADY LILLIAN: Then I shall make mine blisteringly plain: You are welcome in this house only insofar as it would be inhospitable to have you thrown physically from it. Therefore, in the name of decorum, do not force me to ask you to leave immediately. And see that you do so at once.

MILES: Very well. The situation having grown awkward, and your patience thin, I shall take my leave of you. You will, however, have to explain my whereabouts to my wife.

LADY LILLIAN: Don't threaten me! If your wife hears so much as one word of your whereabouts, I shall see to it that you regret every syllable.

(MILLICENT *returns, having composed herself.)*

MILLICENT: Every syllable of what?

LADY LILLIAN: Mrs Monger? What are you doing here?

MILLICENT: Visiting, of course. With my husband.

LADY LILLIAN: Oh. I see. *(She doesn't.)* You could not visit with him at your own residence?

MILLICENT: Ha ha ha! You have the Loveworthy wit, Lady Lillian. My husband is here.

LADY LILLIAN: Yes, apparently. ...And why is that, again?

MILES: As I've already explained, and will, at the risk of redundancy, repeat...

(LORD LOVEWORTHY enters briskly, unannounced.)

LORD LOVEWORTHY: He was invited. And the delightful Mrs. Monger, of course.

(LORD LOVEWORTHY kisses MILLICENT's hand. She giggles and blushes.)

MILLICENT: Oh, Sir Cyril!

(FENNIMORE rushes in, out of breath.)

FENNIMORE: Ahem...Sir Cyril Loveworthy. Lord of the Estate. Knight of the Realm. Man of Letters. *(Panting)* And rather fleet of foot, if I may say so, sir.

LORD LOVEWORTHY: Thank you, Fennimore. *(To* LADY LILLIAN*)* As I am sure he has made every effort to inform you, my dear Lillian, Mister Monger and I have a matter of business to attend to. Haven't we, Miles?

MILES: Certainly, Sir Cyril.

LORD LOVEWORTHY: And as we've seen so little of the Mongers over the many years they have been our next of neighbors, I thought it high time they joined us for high tea. I hope you don't mind, my dear.

LADY LILLIAN: Why should I mind? It is only the latest in a lifetime of impositions that comprise our marriage.

LORD LOVEWORTHY: Ha! Ha! Charming. Mister and Mrs Monger, please, come in, sit down. You must

forgive us for the unconscionable delay in greeting you.
You did find it unconscionable, I hope?

MILLICENT: Not at all.

MILES: Well...

MILLICENT: Not the least bit.

LORD LOVEWORTHY: You see, I have just this morning
completed the manuscript for a new novel, and became
so caught up in the preparation for publication that
I utterly neglected to inform my wife of your coming.
And for that she apologizes.

LADY LILLIAN: I? What have I done?

LORD LOVEWORTHY: Well, I can only assume that you
would assume, upon finding a strange man and his
enchanting wife in our parlour, that they were either
unwelcome intruders, or traveling magicians, and
greeted them with all due disrespect.

LADY LILLIAN: Nonsense. Miles and Millicent are not
strangers. They are our near neighbors. And dear
friends. (It is Millicent, isn't it?) And if my reception
has made either of them feel less than wholeheartedly
welcome, then they have wholly misconstrued.

MILLICENT: Not at all, Lady Lillian. You have been
perfectly gracious, as always. We couldn't be happier
with our reception, could we, Miles?

MILES: Of course not. And if we could—

MILLICENT: Miles!

MILES: I am speaking strictly in the hypothetical.

MILLICENT: I wish you wouldn't.

MILES: Had we been less than well-received,
the oversight was doubtless due to an honest
miscommunication, which could have come between

any pair of spouses. (And I'll thank you not to "Miles" me, Millicent.)

LORD LOVEWORTHY: Very good. Now my dear Lillian, if you would do me the further favour of entertaining Mrs Monger alone a moment, I shall try to make short work of this affair with her husband, and rejoin you both in good time.

LADY LILLIAN: I'm sure I don't know what affair you mean.

LORD LOVEWORTHY: I mean, of course, the affair of business to which we alluded earlier. Would you be so kind?

LADY LILLIAN: Certainly, husband. Shall we wait for you in the garden?

LORD LOVEWORTHY: That won't be necessary. It is a spacious parlour. Miles and I shall simply repair to another corner of it to conduct our business. Fennimore?

FENNIMORE: Yes, your Lordship?

LORD LOVEWORTHY: There is a mahogany case on the cedar shelf above the cherry wood desk in the larger of the two studies overlooking the easternmost orchard. Might I trouble you to fetch it here at once?

FENNIMORE: It sounds like something you would do, sir.

LORD LOVEWORTHY: Thank you, Fennimore. *(To* MILES*)* May I offer you a drink, Mister Monger?

MILES: Thank you, no. I consider the consumption of spirits a vulgar vice which weakens the will and unleashes insidious inhibitions of the flesh that hasten one to sin.

LORD LOVEWORTHY: As do I. Cheers! *(He drinks. As he pours himself another, he gestures to a painting on the wall.)* Perhaps you'd prefer instead to enjoy the intoxicating aesthetic elegance of the serene pastoral setting

depicted in this landscape by an imitator of
Gainsborough? Though often attributed to an
imitator of Rubens.

MILES: A small one, perhaps.

(MILES *and* LORD LOVEWORTHY *gaze at the painting.*)

MILES & LORD LOVEWORTHY: Ah...

(*Meanwhile, in another part of the parlour:*)

MILLICENT: It is kind of you to receive us on such short
notice, Lady Lillian.

LADY LILLIAN: Think nothing of it. It is no more than
my duty as host, wherein kindness is a requisite, not
a prerogative.

MILLICENT: Still, I know it must be an imposition.
Miles is prone to bringing home guests unannounced,
as well. Especially when he's been drinking. I find it an
intolerable inconvenience.

LADY LILLIAN: If they were tolerable or convenient,
we could hardly call them "men".

MILLICENT: Ha ha! That's so. If I may say, Lady Lillian,
it's a wonder the two of us have not grown closer
friends, over the years, living only a yard apart.

LADY LILLIAN: Well, it's a very large yard.

MILLICENT: Yes, I'm winded just from the ride over.
Still, one would think we ought to have so much in
common. Your husband, for example.

LADY LILLIAN: You don't mean to suggest that we
share my husband?

MILLICENT: No, of course not. However, I am a great
fan of his work. And you...well, you married him.

LADY LILLIAN: That's as much an antithesis as a
commonality.

MILLICENT: And then there's my husband.

LADY LILLIAN: What of him?

MILLICENT: Well, he and Lord Loveworthy are both of a sort, aren't they?

LADY LILLIAN: They are uniquely themselves, if that's what you mean. And in that respect they are identical.

MILLICENT: Ha ha! And, of course, we share many personal interests as well.

LADY LILLIAN: For example?

MILLICENT: We are both avid readers.

LADY LILLIAN: There, you are mistaken. My husband being a writer, I have long since lost the will to read.

MILLICENT: But you carry a book with you always.

(Indeed, LADY LILLIAN has a small book tucked under her arm even now.)

LADY LILLIAN: Oh, this is no book.

MILLICENT: It bears an uncanny resemblance to one. In a superficial way.

LADY LILLIAN: It is my diary.

MILLICENT: A diary?

LADY LILLIAN: A candid and confidential repository of all my most secret self-confessions.

MILLICENT: Speaking of candor and confidence, I wonder if I might coax a kind of confession from you, myself?

LADY LILLIAN: As you are my guest, Mrs Monger, kindly coax away.

MILLICENT: Why thank you, Lady Lillian, I appreciate that.

LADY LILLIAN: My pleasure.

MILLICENT: Then may I ask you, in all bluntness...

LADY LILLIAN: Yes, Mrs Monger?

MILLICENT: Why do you despise me?

LADY LILLIAN: Oh, my dear Mrs Monger, the question is absurd.

MILLICENT: Is it?

LADY LILLIAN: Of course.

MILLICENT: I am delighted to hear it.

LADY LILLIAN: If I truly despised you, as you seem to suspect I may have given you cause to believe, I would never admit to it, nor the reason for it.

MILLICENT: Why not?

LADY LILLIAN: Naturally, because, I would either assume that you already knew perfectly well wherein you had wronged me, or not knowing, that the torment of wondering would be a penance you richly deserved.

MILLICENT: I see. Then you admit that you do despise me?

LADY LILLIAN: Not in the least. My admission is merely conjectural. If I despised you, which, of course, I do not, it would be absurd of you to ask, for I would inevitably deny it, insisting instead that we were the best of friends. But as we are the best of friends, the question is absurder still as I do not despise you and I must therefore deny it all the more.

MILLICENT: Well, that is a relief, I suppose.

LADY LILLIAN: Of course it is.

MILLICENT: Do you mind if we sit quietly awhile? I am unused to social discourse, and the effort of this conversation, together with the constrictions of this corset, have quite exhausted me.

LADY LILLIAN: Certainly.

(They sit. MILLICENT *opens her book and* LADY LILLIAN *her diary. They read and write, respectively.)*

(Meanwhile, MILES *finishes enjoying the painting:)*

MILES: Refreshing! But now, down to business. Though, in truth, I haven't the least idea what that business may be.

LORD LOVEWORTHY: Yet you seconded me without hesitation.

MILES: Of course I did. It is a point of honour among gentleman to offer an alibi where one is lacking, and bear witness when none is forthcoming. I am a visitor in your house, Sir Cyril, it would not have been proper to contradict you in front of the ladies.

LORD LOVEWORTHY: Ironic, isn't it? That a husband is more apt to let his wife believe he has business she knows nothing about, than to first know the business himself.

MILES: Very true. But you may dispel the irony by telling me what you have in mind.

LORD LOVEWORTHY: Can you not hazard a guess?

MILES: I wouldn't know where to begin. The two of us have so little in common. Aside from being both of us men, gentlemen, countrymen, neighbors, members of our parish, subjects to our Queen and husbands to our wives, I cannot think of two persons with more disparate personalities, habits and interests.

LORD LOVEWORTHY: You have neglected to mention our professions.

MILES: What of that? I am a literary critic. Whereas, you, on quite the other hand, are a novelist.

LORD LOVEWORTHY: We are both engaged in the field of literature.

MILES: That's as much as to say that my wife engages herself in literature because she is an avid reader of books. Or yours because she keeps a diary. The two professions have as much in common as a manufacturer of decorative inkwells and a lumberjack.

LORD LOVEWORTHY: And which of us is the lumberjack in your simile?

MILES: I should think that goes without saying.

LORD LOVEWORTHY: Perhaps it should. Nonetheless, you must concede that the two disciplines are inter-related, however tenuously. Without a novelist, what would you have to criticize?

MILES: A fair point. And without a critic, who would draw attention to the glaring and obvious flaws in your work?

LORD LOVEWORTHY: Ahem... Yes, well, that brings us conveniently round to the matter in question.

MILES: Which is?

LORD LOVEWORTHY: I am in desperate need of a favour, Miles.

MILES: Anything, Sir Cyril, you have but to name it. I am eternally at your service.

LORD LOVEWORTHY: As you know, I have written a new novel.

MILES: And I shall read it the moment it leaves the presses.

LORD LOVEWORTHY: Read it, if you must, but what I need is a good review.

MILES: Out of the question!

LORD LOVEWORTHY: A kind word from you—

MILES: Never! The integrity of my profession precludes anything but an unbiased and unpremeditated opinion. However cruel.

LORD LOVEWORTHY: I thought as much. I would expect no other response from a man of your reputation.

MILES: I'm astounded that you ventured the suggestion.

LORD LOVEWORTHY: I assure you, I would not have, were I not in such dire straits. You see, Mister Monger, I have a daughter.

MILES: That is no reason to compromise the ethical standards of your profession. And more peculiarly, mine.

LORD LOVEWORTHY: Ordinarily, I would be inclined to agree. But, you see, my daughter, being of legal age and sound mind, recently took it upon herself to take a year from her schooling in order to travel abroad. She departed six months ago, on a yearlong sojourn to America, from which she returns today.

MILES: Then you are more in need of an arithmetician than a journalist. For six months is not nearly a year.

LORD LOVEWORTHY: Cunningly calculated. However, as a journalist, I'm sure it has not escaped your attention that the Earl of Exeter is dead.

MILES: The *Times* published his obituary, not six months ago, on nearly the front page. He died peacefully in his sleep, surrounded by loved ones. Of a hunting accident, as I recall.

LORD LOVEWORTHY: His eldest son, the heir to the Earl, departed the next day... for America.

MILES: What a startling coincidence! That the Earl-apparent should embark for the Colonies on essentially the self-same occasion as your daughter.

LORD LOVEWORTHY: Not entirely. You see, the young Earl is in love with my daughter.

MILES: She must be a remarkable girl then. Or quite blonde.

LORD LOVEWORTHY: But the old Earl had for many years forbidden their courtship, considering my daughter to be considerably beneath his son.

MILES: As I'm sure she must be. He is after all a veritable specimen of noble young manhood.

LORD LOVEWORTHY: You've met the junior Earl?

MILES: I have not. But one can only assume being the heir to an Earl that his better parts must outshine hers. It would be his patriotic duty.

LORD LOVEWORTHY: With the unfortunate passing of the father, the son was finally free to pursue his heart's desire without parental oversight.

MILES: Impetuous. I like that in an Earl. And a fox hound. And has he flushed his figurative quarry?

LORD LOVEWORTHY: So it would seem, for we received word only yestermorning that my daughter is returning unexpectedly and newly-engaged from the Americas with her fiancé. That is the reason I have called you to tea.

MILES: Congratulations are in order then. This should be cause for celebration. Not collusion to defraud the reading public.

LORD LOVEWORTHY: I would be more of a mind to celebrate, were I not the father of the prospective bride, and therefore financially culpable for the cost of any ensuing ceremony. It is a customary exorbitance which, at this time, and with considerable embarrassment, I find myself unable to bear.

MILES: That is quite surprising, since to all outward appearances, you are anything but impoverished.

LORD LOVEWORTHY: Those appearances are correct. I am a man of considerable worldly means. Much of it gained, however, through unsavory sources. So unsavory, in fact, that I dare not, in good conscience, sully the sanctity of my daughter's nuptials with the expenditure of such tainted gains.

MILES: I confess I am befuddled to hear a novelist of your preeminence describe the art of devising intricate fictions and subsequently publishing them for profit as "tainted". Not that I would presume to disagree with you, but a man should take pride in his livelihood, however shameful.

LORD LOVEWORTHY: You misunderstand. My legitimate enterprises—the essays and fiction with which you are familiar—are a source of nothing but pride, both personal and professional. They are, however, a source of little in the way of revenue. I have therefore been forced to resort to more questionable means to supplement my income, for literature alone would have left me destitute.

MILES: How is this possible? You are an acclaimed author. Lavishly and repeatedly praised in all the smaller presses. You have been called a national treasure by no less a person than Her Royal Majesty the Queen's Lord Chamberlain's personal secretary.

LORD LOVEWORTHY: Ah, but what the nation treasures, and what it is willing to purchase at market, are separate commodities altogether. As for acclaim, it is true that I have been routinely lauded in all of the more obscure literary journals. But I am never well-regarded by the one critic whose opinion matters most of all. You.

MILES: Me? I am humbled that my humble opinion means so much to you. But I am sure that it is of little consequence to anyone beyond the handful of millions of subscribers to the daily *Times*.

LORD LOVEWORTHY: You are modest.

MILES: Thank you, I consider it my Christian duty.

LORD LOVEWORTHY: But you are shamelessly mistaken. Your opinion carries considerably more weight than men of twice your girth and stature. In fact, to practitioners of my profession, a favourable mention in the *Times* is a virtual guarantor of financial success, and even excess. Careers have been built and broken on the bedrock of your caprice. Yet, to my ongoing chagrin, you never see fit to hold me in your published esteem.

MILES: On the contrary, I reviewed your debut novel quite favourably, not twenty years ago.

LORD LOVEWORTHY: Yes, I daresay it launched my career. But in the two decades since, you have spoken nought but ill of my work in public, in private, and most especially, in print. As a result, my career has effectively foundered. Though I am still widely-read in academic circles, my work is universally shunned by booksellers, and purveyors of popular fiction. And while I shudder to pander, there is little question that one good word from you—in the form of a published critique—would make my new novel an immediate success and I could afford to pay for my daughter's wedding entirely from legitimate monies. And neither she, nor my wife, need ever discover that my general income is largely ill-gotten.

MILES: I can certainly appreciate the perplexity of your quandary, Sir Cyril, but I must persist in resisting your request.

LORD LOVEWORTHY: I thought you might, initially.

MILES: I am confident you will find that to be my answer in the end result, as well. I don't know why you bothered to ask.

LORD LOVEWORTHY: Rest assured, I would not have, were it not that I knew how easily you could be convinced.

MILES: And yet, you have failed to do so.

LORD LOVEWORTHY: Hesitated to do so, yes. But as for failure, I have not yet begun the attempt. I am reluctant, of course, to resort to extortion. But it seems you leave me no choice but to leave you no choice.

MILES: Please, commence to compel me, then, for I find your present state of persuasion, insultingly insufficient.

LORD LOVEWORTHY: Suppose I were to tell you, Miles, that I have a sordid secret which, were I to reveal it, as I shortly shall, would have you so wholly converted to my way of thinking, that knowing now what you will know then, you would, were you then here now, beg yourself to simply give me the money to pay for my daughter's wedding outright and spare us both the indignity of disclosing that which I have thus far refrained from revealing, out of concern for your own well-being and our continued good relations.

MILES: What nonsense! Is this an offer of blackmail? If so, it is poorly managed. Your reasons cannot possibly be so convincing as you contend, or you would divulge them at once and have done with it. I can conceive of no reason for withholding them.

LORD LOVEWORTHY: That is because you have not conceived of my secret, nor the ill-will it will inevitably engender. So, for the time being, and for the sake of an amicable tea, I shall continue to be the sole steward of our mutual respect, while I strive to contrive a more courteous means to broach it.

MILES: As you wish. I trust to your discretion.

(FENNIMORE *returns with the case.*)

FENNIMORE: The mahogany case, sir.

LORD LOVEWORTHY: Thank you, Fennimore.
Mister Monger, are you a gaming man?

MILES: It is a vile habit in which I never indulge,
except of course when the stakes are suitable,
and victory certain.

LORD LOVEWORTHY: Suppose, then, I were to propose
a wager—

MILES: *(Immediately)* Name your stakes!

LORD LOVEWORTHY: —The terms of which would
satisfy my particulars while presenting you with
an incentive short of coercion.

MILES: I am intrigued. Go on.

LORD LOVEWORTHY: My daughter's homeward ship
arrived this morning at Portsmouthsborough with her
fiancé. From thence they will no doubt detour briefly
through Exeter for the afternoon to secure the blessing
of his widowed mother, before coming here for a
nightcap and mine. If, by the time of her arrival here
this evening, I can convince you to change your mind,
you will not only agree to write me the review I require,
but freely offer to pay for the wedding itself out of your
own pocket.

MILES: I see you are no more a gambler than a
blackmailer, for the wager is preposterous. Were you
a humourist, I should think the whole betrothal were
an elaborate and hilarious hoax.

LORD LOVEWORTHY: Perhaps this will convince you of
the veracity of the situation: Fennimore, the case...

(FENNIMORE *opens the case, revealing a pair of finely-crafted dueling pistols.*)

MILES: What's this? Dueling pistols? Are you threatening me?

LORD LOVEWORTHY: It certainly adds a degree of urgency, don't you think? I have an acquaintance in Russia, a playwright of some regional renown, who is fond of saying that one does not introduce a firearm into the first act of a play, without firing the same in the second. Or the fourth, I forget.

MILES: I don't see what that has to do with the present situation.

LORD LOVEWORTHY: Little, if anything, I'm sure.

MILES: Then what is the point? Why show me this?

LORD LOVEWORTHY: These are Loveworthy family heirlooms. They were once used by my grandfather to fend off a marauding boar who had wandered into the master bedroom, if my grandfather's stories are to be believed. Or a rutting pig in the pantry, if the kitchen help is to be believed.

MILES: And which am I in this metaphor?

LORD LOVEWORTHY: Neither, I should hope. You misunderstand me entirely.

MILES: You attempt to coerce compensation from me under threat of purported blackmail, and then regale me with your family history for exterminating swine and I'm not to take it as either insult or intimidation? Or both??

LORD LOVEWORTHY: That was not my intent.

MILES: How dare you, sir! How dare you! And if you were not presently armed, I should reprimand you in less uncertain terms.

(LADY LILLIAN *and* MILLICENT *hurry over to see what the commotion is.)*

LADY LILLIAN: What is the matter?

MILLICENT: We heard voices raised in umbrage.

MILES: Your husband, Lady Loveworthy, has threatened me!

LADY LILLIAN: Bodily? Or with his dagger-like wit?

LORD LOVEWORTHY: I have done nothing of the sort.

MILES: See for yourself!

(MILES *shows them the case of dueling pistols. The ladies gasp.)*

LADY LILLIAN: Dueling pistols! In the house?

LORD LOVEWORTHY: They are a gift for our daughter's fiancé. The ex-Earl of Exeter was an accomplished marksman. A family tradition he has passed down to his son. I had them engraved.

LADY LILLIAN: *(Reading)* "To my beloved daughter and her soon-to-be-beloved fiancé on the occasion of their engagement: 'A right fair mark, fair Earl, is soonest hit'."

MILES: Ah. Tasteful, but ribald. A thoughtful engagement gift. My compliments.

LORD LOVEWORTHY: You see, Lillian? A simple misunderstanding.

LADY LILLIAN: Misunderstanding or no, I will not have pistols in the parlour. You'll frighten the guests.

MILES: I am not frightened, rest assured. I served in the Infantry, after all.

LORD LOVEWORTHY: Be reasonable, Lillian.

LADY LILLIAN: I shall have my reason restored when these weapons have been removed from the house. You

know what happened to your grandfather. Millie, will
you come with me? We shall take them into the garden.

LORD LOVEWORTHY: Why must you both go?

LADY LILLIAN: Because no married woman should
be left alone with a firearm. The temptation is simply
too great.

MILLICENT: I will come with you, Lady Lillian.
(To MILES*)* Shame on you, Miles.

MILES: I—!?

LADY LILLIAN: Fennimore!

FENNIMORE: Yes, my Lady?

LADY LILLIAN: Gather up the pistols, we are taking
them into the garden.

FENNIMORE: Yes, my Lady.

*(*FENNIMORE *does.* LADY LILLIAN *and* MILLICENT *go with
him.)*

LORD LOVEWORTHY: If I frightened you, I, of course,
apologize.

MILES: Not at all. It was a minor misunderstanding
between gentlemen which the women have elevated
to hysterics, as is the bent of their gender. A set of
dueling pistols is a gift which I'm sure any newly-
engaged couple would be proud to own and perhaps
even find use for.

LORD LOVEWORTHY: I knew you would understand.

MILES: You asked me before if I were a gambling man,
but it appears you are not yourself availed of that vice.

LORD LOVEWORTHY: Why do you say that?

MILES: Well, as I mentioned, the wager you propose is
preposterous.

LORD LOVEWORTHY: How so?

MILES: There are no stakes. What is to be gained?

LORD LOVEWORTHY: If you win, you spare yourself the cost of a very expensive wedding.

MILES: An expense I could easily evade by declining to accept the wager in the first place. Where is my enticement to take a risk at all?

LORD LOVEWORTHY: Ah! A good point. You are correct, I am a novice at gaming. The stakes should be equal. But you don't have a daughter.

MILES: True.

LORD LOVEWORTHY: I could give you the equivalent in banknotes.

MILES: The equivalent of a daughter?

LORD LOVEWORTHY: Of a daughter's wedding.

MILES: There again is an inherent inequity. The amount in question means little to a man of your exorbitant wealth, whereas the cost of providing a wedding fit for an Earl, or any member of the British nobility, could bankrupt a man of my moderate means.

LORD LOVEWORTHY: How would you frame it, then?

MILES: Hmm... Aha! I have it! If you cannot convince me, by the time of your daughter's arrival on these premises today, to give your new novel an undeservedly favourable review: You will relinquish your quill and retire forever from the field of fiction.

LORD LOVEWORTHY: You would ruin me?

MILES: Equivalency, your Lordship! It would ruin you no more than it would my own reputation should your novel prove to be too obviously undeserving of the praise I am expected to lavish upon it. I, too, could be ruined by the stakes of this wager. Thus, we have a proposition that is a precipitous gamble for both of us.

LORD LOVEWORTHY: Point taken. Still, it demonstrates a cruelty on your part, which I would not have expected in a church-going man.

MILES: A common misconception. The commandments have never precluded cruelty from their ten tenets.

LORD LOVEWORTHY: Very well. Since I am certain to win, I accept your terms.

MILES: Done! Though how you expect to convince me of something that is now firmly against my own financial interest, I cannot imagine.

LORD LOVEWORTHY: That is because you are a critic. Your imagination is purely derivative, whereas the challenge of concocting hitherto unforeseen scenarios is my stock in trade, and one I relish daily. Let us have a toast to seal the bargain.

(FENNIMORE *has entered.*)

LORD LOVEWORTHY: Fennimore! Oh, here you are.

FENNIMORE: Sir—

LORD LOVEWORTHY: Two of my finest cognac.

FENNIMORE: But sir—

LORD LOVEWORTHY: At once, Fennimore! This is a momentous occasion, it requires immediate brandy.

FENNIMORE: Yes, sir. (*He exits.*)

LORD LOVEWORTHY: What shall we drink to?

MILES: To your daughter's timely arrival, of course. When did you say she is expected?

(EMILY *bursts in, unannounced.*)

EMILY: Daddy!

(FENNIMORE *returns with two snifters of brandy.*)

FENNIMORE: Ahem... The young Miss Emily
Loveworthy, scholar, traveller and Daughter of the
House. Returned prematurely from America.

EMILY: What a glorious day!

MILES: Glorious, indeed. Cheers! *(He drinks.)*

END OF ACT ONE

ACT TWO
The American Fiancé

(Scene: The parlour of Loveworthy Manor.)

(LADY LILLIAN and MILLICENT hurry in from the garden.)

LADY LILLIAN: Emily!

MILLICENT: The Loveworthys' daughter!

(Enter EARL, unshaven and hairy, with a mangy fur cap, carrying EMILY's luggage.)

FENNIMORE: Ahem... And a scruffy baggage handler.

EMILY: Oh, no, Fennimore, this man is my fiancé, not my valet. *(To EARL)* Put them over there.

MILLICENT: *(To MILES)* Did she say, "fiancé"?

MILES: *(To MILLICENT)* Did she say "man"?

LADY LILLIAN: Do I smell haggis?

EMILY: Earl, I'd like you to meet my mother, the Lady Lillian Loveworthy, and my father, Sir Cyril, about both of whom you've heard so much you must find meeting them almost superfluous. And Father, Mother, I would like you to meet my fiancé—

LADY LILLIAN: We will do no such thing!

LORD LOVEWORTHY: I demand an explanation, young lady! As does your mother!

LADY LILLIAN: What is the meaning of this?

EMILY: I daresay it is not my meaning which is obscure.

LADY LILLIAN: Oh! Cyril?

LORD LOVEWORTHY: Emily! Your manners! I don't know what incivility your Colonial sojourn has taught you, but you are home now and I'll thank you to show your mother less cheek in her immediate presence.

EARL: And I'll thank you to show my fiancé some o' the same in mine.

LORD LOVEWORTHY: Your fiancé is nonetheless my daughter, sir, and I hope your engagement does not preclude my continuing to address her in whatsoever manner I deem appropriately paternal, as I have done throughout her life, and shall continue to do throughout the remainder of mine, however foreshortened it may be by the strains she contrives to place upon my heart.

EMILY: Oh!

EARL: Now, see here—!

LORD LOVEWORTHY: (Diplomatically) However... You are entirely correct to counsel public discretion in such private matters. I shall therefore restrain myself from further such outbursts, in your presence, in future.

EARL: Thank you.

LORD LOVEWORTHY: (Perfunctorily) Emily, my dear, welcome. It is a delight to see you home. Would you be so kind as to accompany your mother and myself into the garden?

EARL: What—?

LORD LOVEWORTHY: There is a pressing matter of familial urgency which warrants our immediate attention, discussion, and some privacy.

EMILY: Oh, of course, Father.

EARL: But Emily—!

EMILY: It's all right, darling. I'm sure this won't take but a moment, whatever it is.

LORD LOVEWORTHY: Mister and Mrs. Monger, would it trouble you terribly to play host to our guest in the brief interim of our imminent absence?

LADY LILLIAN: An absence which will no doubt be made fonder by the cucumber sandwiches Fennimore is presently bringing in from the pantry. Fennimore!

(FENNIMORE *enters with a tray full of cucumber sandwiches.*

FENNIMORE: Ahem...sandwiches of cucumber and clotted cream on rye toast with garnish of coriander sprig.

EARL: What's coriander?

FENNIMORE: If you have to ask, you are too smelly.

EMILY: Fennimore!

MILLICENT: We will afford the young man every courtesy we would a visitor in our own house.

LADY LILLIAN: If you could afford him a few courtesies more, I'd appreciate it. This is a considerably larger house.

LORD LOVEWORTHY: I am sure the Mongers will do their utmost to host our guest as best befits.

MILES: It will be our pleasure.

LORD LOVEWORTHY: I will esteem it a great personal favour.

MILES: No more than it will be an honour and a privilege to be of such service, Sir Cyril.

LORD LOVEWORTHY: I am indebted to you.

MILES: And I to you. (Though not literally, if I may take a moment to gloat.)

LORD LOVEWORTHY: As I shall be out of earshot, you may gloat till you are glutted. Emily, the garden!

(LADY LILLIAN *gives* EMILY *a little shove.*)

EMILY: Oh!

(LORD LOVEWORTHY, LADY LILLIAN *and* EMILY *exit into the garden.*)

MILLICENT: Well, this is indeed a rare honour. An Earl in our house.

MILES: He is not in our house, Millicent. It is the Loveworthys' estate.

MILLICENT: Wherein the Loveworthys have asked us to play host.

MILES: It is idiocy to take the request literally.

MILLICENT: If you think it idiocy to receive an Earl in one's home...

MILES: I think nothing of the sort. (*To* EARL, *sycophantically*) It is indeed an inordinate honour. One of which we, and indeed even the Loveworthys, are not entirely worthy. (*To* MILLICENT) But it is imbecilic to pretend that it is actually happening!

MILLICENT: I am sure the good Earl does not consider his visitation imbecilic.

EARL: Um... Yes. Nice to be here.

MILLICENT: Oh, of course it is. You've just popped in from America, of all places.

EARL: Well, there was a pretty long boat ride first.

MILES: A boat? Oho! I must compliment you, Earl. You have mastered the accent.

EARL: What accent is that?

MILES: The American accent.

MILLICENT: You sound positively Colonial.

EARL: Thank you, I suppose.

MILES: How have you done it?

EARL: ...With my mouth?

MILES: Ah, the American wit. I see you've acquired that, as well. I've heard so much about it: Wry. Paradoxical. Humourous, albeit in the abstract. Well done, sir. Very amusing.

MILLICENT: Tell us another.

EARL: ...Another what?

(They stare at EARL *blankly, then to be polite, burst out laughing. Then...)*

MILES: We were very sorry to hear about your father.

MILLICENT: Yes.

EARL: Why? What have you heard?

MILES: Well... The news, of course.

EARL: News about my father?

MILLICENT: Yes.

EARL: Here in England?

MILES: Yes.

EARL: What is it?

MILES: The news?

EARL: Yes.

MILES: Don't you know?

EARL: No. Would you kindly tell me?

MILES: Oh, no. That wouldn't be kind at all.

EARL: Why not?

MILES: I thought you already knew. I thought that's why you left for America.

EARL: Left where for America?

MILES: England.

EARL: I've yet to leave England for anyplace.

MILLICENT: You never left?

MILES: You mean the entire time you've been overseas, you've been here in England all along?

EARL: I have never been anywhere overseas, *except* England.

(They stare at EARL *blankly, then burst out laughing.)*

EARL: What have you heard about my father?!

MILES: Oh. Oh, that. Oh, I really don't think I should be the one to broach it to you. It wouldn't be appropriate.

EARL: Well, somebody better start broaching, or things are going to get mighty inappropriate in here.

MILES: You are right, of course. Millicent!

MILLICENT: What?

MILES: You'd better tell him.

MILLICENT: Me?

MILES: He has a right to know.

EARL: Know *what*?!

MILES: Yes, Millicent, get to the point.

MILLICENT: Oh, my dear Earl... Oh, this is very upsetting. It's your father...

EARL: I gathered. What about him?

MILLICENT: I'm afraid he has passed.

EARL: Passed what?

MILLICENT: ...On.

EARL: You mean he's dead?

MILLICENT: *(Relieved)* Yes, thank you.

EARL: That's the news?

MILES: Millicent is sorry to be the one to tell you.

MILLICENT: I am.

MILES: Faster next time, Millicent.

EARL: But I already knew that.

MILES: You did?

EARL: I was there when it happened.

MILES: At his bedside with the family, of course!
Or were you there for the hunting accident?

EARL: That was no accident. It was an ambush.

MILES: An ambush? In Exeter?

EARL: My father was leading a wagon train through
Pike's Pass in winter when we were set upon by a band
of Mormons dressed as Indians. I was only thirteen at
the time. And being neither an adult male, nor a girl
of any age, was neither killed on the spot, nor taken off
to wife. But my father, may he rest in peace, was cut to
pieces in that pass. And to this day there's not a night
goes by but I wake screaming at the memory of his
dismemberment.

(They stare at EARL blankly, then burst into polite laughter.)

MILES: Delightfully ironic.

MILLICENT: And not at all disturbing.

EARL: I don't mean to be rude—

MILLICENT: Of course you don't.

MILES: It would be beneath you.

MILLICENT: A man of your breeding.

EARL: —But who the blazes are you?

MILES: Ah! You see, Millicent, what happens when one is not properly introduced? I am, of course, Miles Monger, the chief literary critic for the *Times* of London. And this is my wife Millicent. But you may call her Mrs Monger.

MILLICENT: Or he can call me Millie, if he likes.

MILES: I'm sure the Earl will call you whatsoever he pleases. And you will answer to it whether you like it or no. *(To* EARL*)* Unless of course you'd rather not.

EARL: Um...no...Millie's fine.

MILES: Millicent and I are the Loveworthys' adjacent neighbors. We are practically family.

MILLICENT: And therefore practically in-laws.

EARL: Oh.

*(*FENNIMORE *enters.)*

FENNIMORE: Ahem... The Loveworthys: Lord and Lady, and their daughter Emily, in tears.

(The LOVEWORTHYS *return.* EMILY *is in tears.)*

EARL: What? Emily?

LORD LOVEWORTHY: Thank you all for your patient indulgence. As I had suspected, the matter was easily and happily resolved. Emily!

*(*EMILY *stops sobbing.)*

LORD LOVEWORTHY: I hope in the meantime you have not been troubled overmuch by the crude company.

MILLICENT: Not at all, we were quite well-behaved.

MILES: Speak for yourself.

LORD LOVEWORTHY: I mean of course *his* crude company.

(LORD LOVEWORTHY *turns accusingly to* EARL.)

EARL: What have *I* done?

LORD LOVEWORTHY: Don't think that I won't tell you precisely what you've done.

LADY LILLIAN: And had you any decency, you would confess it openly and spare us all the impending exposition.

EARL: I'm sure I don't know what you're talking about.

LORD LOVEWORTHY: Indeed you do! Though you may not know it yet. For, having conferred with my daughter in private, per your suggestion, I can now say what I could not in good conscience have presumed to assume of someone whose acquaintance I had only just made.

EARL: Which is?

LORD LOVEWORTHY: That you, sir, are an impostor!

EARL: What?

MILES: He's not the Earl of Exeter?

LORD LOVEWORTHY: He is no Earl at all!

LADY LILLIAN: He does not even have the decency to be British.

LORD LOVEWORTHY: And worse yet, he's an American.

MILES: My God!

EARL: Yes, I am. And I never claimed to be anything else.

MILLICENT: And you're not an Earl, either, as you pretended?

EARL: I did no such thing.

MILES: Indeed you did, sir. Indeed you did.

EARL: When?

MILES: Just now, when my wife and I quite naturally assumed you to be of noble birth, despite all appearances to the contrary. And you quite deceitfully failed to deny it. Or make any attempt to dissuade us of our mispresumptions.

EARL: How was I to know what kinda presumptions you made about me without my knowing? This is ridiculous! Emily?

EMILY: Yes, darling?

MILES: Don't seek to draw this poor hapless girl any further into your lattice of lies. You have made a fool of her, and of my gullible wife and I shall not stand for it in my house.

MILLICENT: The Loveworthys are back, dear. It's their house again.

MILES: In my neighborhood then. Or my parish. Nay, my country! How dare you sully the flower of English maidenhood, and the vine-ripened fruit of English matronhood, with your deceptions? Were you not a strapping young man, I should make bold to slap you. And you, young lady: Were I not confident, by your tearful entrance, that your father had already upbraided you for your unwitting role in this subterfuge, I should certainly inform you that you ought to be ashamed.

MILLICENT: (Kindly) He's right, dear, shame on you.

EARL: That's enough! I have never been so insulted in my life! And I've been to Nebraska!

LADY LILLIAN: Hence, the stench.

LORD LOVEWORTHY: I thought something smelt of agriculture.

EMILY: Father, Mother, Mongers! You're behaving deplorably toward the man who intends to make me his bride.

LORD LOVEWORTHY: His intentions notwithstanding, he shall do no such thing under my roof. And as you are never leaving the house again without armed escort, he is not likely to do so elsewhere either.

EMILY: Father—

LORD LOVEWORTHY: No, Emily.

EMILY: Mother—?

LADY LILLIAN: Ask your father.

EMILY: But— Oh, this is dreadful. Dreadful! I shall pout. *(She does.)*

LORD LOVEWORTHY: How could you, Emily? Think how your impetuousness has dashed your poor mother's hopes of a promising match.

LADY LILLIAN: When you wrote to say you were marrying an Earl, we quite naturally assumed that you would be marrying...an Earl.

EMILY: But I am.

EARL: She is.

LORD LOVEWORTHY: We have already established that this man is no Earl, as he is American, and they haven't the class.

EARL: The Americans have me. And I am Earl Kant.

LORD LOVEWORTHY: What did you call me?

EMILY: I wrote to you that I was marrying an Earl, because I did not, at the time, know his full name— the romance has been a bit of a whirlwind—but now that I have come to know him better, I can tell you his

name is Earl Kant, and he is a respected American
entrepreneur and saloon keeper from Flagstaff, Arizona.

MILES: Respected and American? There's a singular
oxymoron.

LADY LILLIAN: But Emily, I don't understand. The real
Earl of Exeter departed for America months ago in
pursuit of his schoolhood sweetheart, to find you,
woo you, and win your hand.

EMILY: But I never liked him. Not in school or any other
place. He was always a terrible boor and a drunkard.

LORD LOVEWORTHY: You cannot begrudge the boy
being Irish.

MILES: If he had his vices, I'm sure it was out of respect
for his heritage.

EMILY: I left school to travel abroad in hopes of
avoiding his unscholastic advances. I cannot help
it if he followed me there unbidden.

LORD LOVEWORTHY: Be that as it may, I, for one, and
I'm not alone, should like to know how, given the
choice and opportunity, you ended up with the likes
of this fellow, when the very flower and bastion of
English nobility was knocking at your door. Or tent
flap. Or whatever you dwelt behind over there.

EMILY: He was no flower, trust me.

EARL: But he was kind of a bastion.

MILES: And where is he? It is not like an Earl, and a
marksman, to become lost upon a strange continent
without sending home word of his exploits, and a
shipment of exotic pelts.

EARL: I can answer you that: Your precious Earl is not
lost at all. He's still in Flagstaff.

LADY LILLIAN: Oh, it's worse than we thought.

LORD LOVEWORTHY: What is he doing there?

EARL: Rotting in an open grave, as far as I know.
Unless the coyotes got to him.

MILES: An open grave?!

EARL: But the coyotes probably got to him.

LADY LILLIAN: You mean he's dead?!

EARL: And all but buried.

LADY LILLIAN: Are you sure of it?

EARL: As sure as I can be having shot him myself.

LORD LOVEWORTHY: You what?!

EARL: I shot him.

MILES: You shot him? You murdered an Earl??

EARL: I'd have killed a Duke for what he done.

MILES: Don't say that! It's treason!

LADY LILLIAN: This is a respectable house.

EMILY: Before you leap to misjudgment and
overreaction, you may wish to know Earl's reason
for so doing.

LORD LOVEWORTHY: What possible reason could there
be for assassinating a newly-minted member of the
British peerage?

EARL: I'll have you know, he mistreated Emily very
badly.

EMILY: I nearly have bruises.

EARL: He showed up at the saloon where she worked.
And when she refused his unwanted attentions,
he became surly and drunk.

EMILY: No, he was already drunk.

LADY LILLIAN: You worked in a saloon??

LORD LOVEWORTHY: Emily, work? How could you?

EARL: Once drunk, he openly reviled her. Publicly disparaging her character, her parentage—

EMILY: And my hair.

LADY LILLIAN: That was uncalled for.

EARL: So I took it upon myself to defend her honour. And, by extension, yours.

EMILY: And my hair.

MILES: But the Earl of Exeter was a master gunsman. You could not possibly have bested him in a gun battle.

EARL: A fact he made us all aware of with his endless boasts and braggardry. And demonstrations of trick marksmanship.

EMILY: There wasn't a playing card in the place without a bullet hole through the center. Or a coin above a nickel. It was annoying, really.

EARL: So I challenged him to a duel.

MILES: Ha ha ha!

EARL: And while he was doubled over with laughter, I shot him in the back.

MILES: Oh!

LADY LILLIAN & MILLICENT: Oh!!

EARL: Then I beat him with a bar stool till he quit twitching.

MILES, LADY LILLIAN & MILLICENT: Oh!!!

LORD LOVEWORTHY: How ungentlemanly!

EARL: If it's the gentlemanly custom to defend a lady's honour badly, then I give you I'm no gentlemen.

EMILY: So you see, Father, Earl shot—and subsequently bludgeoned—the Earl out of respect for me. Naturally, I was smitten.

MILES: This is disgraceful! You, sir, are a disgrace! And I say that in my critical capacity, not as any kind of physical threat.

LORD LOVEWORTHY: And you, Emily, taking up with a common thug and a murderer?

EMILY: Oh, he is hardly common. Earl is the most noble man I have ever had the privilege to have known.

LORD LOVEWORTHY: Then you would do well with looking up "nobility" in a dictionary. Fennimore!

LADY LILLIAN: Emily, this is entirely unacceptable. Did I not think you had been raised better I should suspect you were marrying him out of sheer rebellion.

LORD LOVEWORTHY: We shall have to fire those nannies.

EMILY: It is not Migdalia's fault that I am poorly parented!

LADY LILLIAN: I hope you're not trying to blame poor Fennimore for this.

EMILY: Oh, you are impossible!

LORD LOVEWORTHY: If this is to be one of your tantrums, I shall have to ask you to go to your room.

EARL: And I shall have to ask you, sir—

LORD LOVEWORTHY: And I shall ask you!

MILES: And I shall second his ask-ance, so there's no chance of you creeping at him from behind. (To LORD LOVEWORTHY) Shall I have Fennimore fetch the pistols from the garden?

LADY LILLIAN: Enough! I'll have no more talk of men and their guns in this house. Let us have some tea.

There's been enough unpleasantness on an empty stomach for one afternoon. Fennimore!

(FENNIMORE *enters with a dictionary.*)

FENNIMORE: Ahem... Nobility! Noun! A class of persons distinguished by high birth or rank.

LADY LILLIAN: No, Fennimore, tea! The tea!

FENNIMORE: Noun! An aromatic, slightly bitter beverage—

LADY LILLIAN: No, the tea itself, bring it!

FENNIMORE: Yes, milady. (*He goes and returns shortly with tea.*)

LADY LILLIAN: Cyril, as much as it chagrins me to be even in the presence of such pungent company— (*To* EARL) What animal is that, by the way?

(LADY LILLIAN *indicates his fur cap.*)

EARL: It's part sheepdog, part border collie.

LORD LOVEWORTHY: You skinned a mongrel to make a hat?

EARL: No, I skinned a couple purebreds to make jerky. And what's left of 'em we made into hats.

EMILY: I have one, too. (*She puts on a matching dog-skin cap.*)

EMILY: Mine's spaniel and bloodhound.

LADY LILLIAN: Ugh. Positively revolting! Nevertheless, decorum dictates that we maintain our couth. Even if our guest cannot.

LORD LOVEWORTHY: You are right, my dear. Mister Kant, I must apologize if our earlier exchange became heated or churlish. It was tactless of me to stoop to your level.

EARL: Um...

EMILY: *(Nudging him)* Apology accepted.

EARL: Right.

FENNIMORE: Ahem... Tea?

EARL: Thank you.

LADY LILLIAN: And have you tried the cucumber sandwiches?

EARL: They're delicious.

LADY LILLIAN: Thank you. I had Fennimore make them myself.

FENNIMORE: Crumpet?

EMILY: No, thank you.

FENNIMORE: Tart?

EMILY: No, thank you.

FENNIMORE: Trollop?

EMILY: I'm not hungry, Fennimore.

LADY LILLIAN: Now, isn't this more civilized?

ALL: *Mm-hmm.*

LADY LILLIAN: *(To* LORD LOVEWORTHY*)* Quickly, dear, make conversation, before a lull sets in.

LORD LOVEWORTHY: Mister Kant!

EARL: Yes, sir?

LORD LOVEWORTHY: Now that the initial awkwardness of discovering you to be a blood-thirsty butcher has passed: I must admit, your interest in my daughter piques my own in you. For a man of your obvious ilk, it seems inexplicably audacious to assume that you might aspire in marriage to a lady of Emily's caliber.

LADY LILLIAN: I said no talk of guns.

LORD LOVEWORTHY: I apologize, dear. It seems to me that you are either a remarkably courageous fellow. Or some sort of sociopath.

EMILY: Oh, the former, Father. You must not judge a man by his outward appearances. Or their smell.

LADY LILLIAN: *(Aside to* LORD LOVEWORTHY*)* You know, Cyril, your half-brother's step-daughter, Eugenia, has no olfactory organs.

LORD LOVEWORTHY: That's true, she lost them in that threshing accident.

LADY LILLIAN: And her recent correspondence hinted that she was open to offers of courtship, however desperate.

LORD LOVEWORTHY: Mister Kant, out of curiosity: What were your intentions toward our daughter?

EARL: Completely honourable, I assure you.

LORD LOVEWORTHY: Your assurances notwithstanding, I must insist on particulars.

EARL: Well, you see...I love her.

LADY LILLIAN: Oh!

MILLICENT: Oh my!

LADY LILLIAN: Mister Kant, this is neither a bawdy house, nor a seaport. If you are going to air your amorous predilections, we must repair this discussion to the garden.

EARL: Yes, ma'am.

LORD LOVEWORTHY: Go on, Mister Kant.

EARL: She is beautiful beyond words.

LORD LOVEWORTHY: That goes without saying.

EMILY: Touché.

LORD LOVEWORTHY: What else?

MILES: Oh, this is futility! We all know what he sees in her. She is an attractive, vivacious, nubile virgin of reasonable means and British citizenship. Why, were I twenty years younger and foreign, I should try my hand at her affections myself.

MILLICENT: Twenty years ago, you were already married to me, Miles.

MILES: Well, yes, and I was already British. But were I neither, here is an appealing means to both ends.

MILLICENT: I would have been British twenty years ago.

MILES: Oh, you know what I mean! The question before us is not what he sees in her. But what she could possibly see in him!

LORD LOVEWORTHY: Well put. How say you, Mister Kant?

EARL: I'm afraid you'll have to ask the lady. I don't pretend to speak for her.

LADY LILLIAN: Adorable.

LORD LOVEWORTHY: Yes. Well, Emily, since your fiancé hasn't the decency to spare you direct inquiry, you shall have to tell us yourself: What is the attraction?

EMILY: Well, you see...I love him.

MILLICENT: Oh!

LADY LILLIAN: Not this again.

EMILY: He has the soul of an artist.

LORD LOVEWORTHY: That is as much as to say Miles has the soul of a swashbuckler. It may be true, but it does not make him a pirate. Nor put him any further out to sea.

LADY LILLIAN: It matters very little if a man has the soul of anything if he has not the vessel of one as well.

EMILY: Will it suffice that he has the parlour of one?

LORD LOVEWORTHY: Of an artist?

EMILY: Yes.

LORD LOVEWORTHY: I apologize then, for my preemptive sarcasm, Mister Kant. I assumed, of course, that Emily was being figurative in her praise. Are you, in fact, a creative artisan of some stripe?

EARL: Yes. I suppose I am.

LORD LOVEWORTHY: Indeed? What is your medium?

EARL: I guess you could say... Flesh.

(MILES *leaps out of his seat, his tea clattering offendedly to the floor.*)

MILES: Oh! I have not the slightest idea what that means but it is thoroughly repulsive! There are ladies present, sir. And gentlemen.

EMILY: It means, Mister Monger, that he is a tattooist. Earl owns a parlour in Flagstaff.

LADY LILLIAN: A tattooing parlour?

EARL: Yes, ma'am.

EMILY: He owns a number of establishments: A saloon. A barbershop. The general store.

EARL: Bait shop.

EMILY: He is also a tobacconist.

LADY LILLIAN: *(Impressed)* A tobacconist? How exotic!

LORD LOVEWORTHY: Ah! The American weed. I have heard so much about it.

MILES: I hear it clears the lungs and sharpens the wits.

EARL: Yes, that's what we tell the dim-witted.

MILES: They say it's all the rage in Bensonhedge.

LORD LOVEWORTHY: It sounds terribly refreshing.

MILES: Have you brought any with you?

EARL: Would you like to try it?

MILES: Yes, yes, please!

EARL: Emily, will you fetch the roll of buckskins from my bag? The cigarettes ought to be in it.

EMILY: Here it is.

(EARL unfurls the roll of buckskins. LORD LOVEWORTHY and MILES recoil in disgust.)

MILES & LORD LOVEWORTHY: *Oh!*

EARL: No, that's the bait. Look in the skunk-skin rucksack.

EMILY: Here they are.

(EMILY takes out a packet of rolled cigarettes and hands one to each of the men: LORD LOVEWORTHY, MILES, FENNIMORE and EARL. Then she lights them.)

LADY LILLIAN: *(To MILLICENT)* Boys and their foibles.

(EMILY lights herself a cigarette, as well. They smoke.)

LORD LOVEWORTHY: As I thought: Terribly refreshing!

MILES: And exhilarating!

FENNIMORE: Asphyxiating!

EMILY: And sophisticated!

LADY LILLIAN: Emily!

EMILY: What?

LADY LILLIAN: What in the name of God's heaven do you think you are doing with that cigarette?

EMILY: I suspect I am smoking it.

LADY LILLIAN: Not in this house you are not!

LORD LOVEWORTHY: Put that down at once, Emily!
It is a deplorable habit!

EMILY: You're doing it!

LORD LOVEWORTHY: I am doing it in the dignified
manner of a refined English gentleman. You are doing
it in the lewd fashion of a scurvy French serving wench.

EMILY: We're doing it exactly the same.

LADY LILLIAN: Your father is not wearing crinolines.

EMILY: This is the height of hypocrisy. Why must the
rules of civil society differ so inexplicably for men as
for their female counterparts?

MILES: A woman is not a counterpart to anything. She
is an helpmeet, first and foremost. And a temptation to
sin, second.

MILLICENT: As you'll discover on your wedding night.

EMILY: This may come as a societal shock to you, but in
the Americas, a woman may do anything a man can do,
if she has the gumption for it. And a big enough gun.

EARL: And plenty of ammunition.

LADY LILLIAN: There is the fallacy in your argument,
for no woman worth her wiles would willingly wield a
weapon, no matter how effectively it satisfied her ends.

MILLICENT: Or her midsection.

LORD LOVEWORTHY: Had I known you would return
from the States thoroughly Frenchified, I would never
have permitted you to leave Europe.

LADY LILLIAN: I told you we should have sent her to
Paris. At least there the perversions are clearly labeled,
in a language she does not understand.

MILES: If I may say, Lord Loveworthy, this is what comes of associating with entrepreneurs. Money should never be earned, when it can be inherited. Hard work may seem a virtue, in theory, but in practice, a life of industry leads to indulging in one's own wares. Fraternizing with a tobacconist has led your daughter to smoke. Smoking with a tattooist may lead her Lord knows where.

LORD LOVEWORTHY: Mister Monger is correct, Emily. Next, you'll be wanting a tattoo.

EMILY: Yes, I shall! For I already do.

LADY LILLIAN: Want a tattoo?

MILLICENT: Emily, your body is your temple.

EMILY: And that's why I've chosen to erect it a crucifix, here on my ankle. Or a dolphin. I haven't decided.

LORD LOVEWORTHY: Earl, you cannot allow this. Surely, even a man such as yourself would not let his future bride disfigure herself in an act of misguided piety. And/or zoology.

EARL: Disfigurement is in the eye of the beholder, sir. As is piety. Some would consider the procedure an enhancement.

LORD LOVEWORTHY: And those most likely to applaud the improvement are those who would profit by the renovation. No doubt it is your tattoo parlour wherein she intends to be besmirched?

EARL: Yes, of course.

LORD LOVEWORTHY: So you admit that you may be predisposed to condone her indiscretion?

EARL: I submit that I may be the only one here without a preconceived bias against the fleshy art.

LADY LILLIAN: Please, don't call it that.

EARL: But if it eases your indignation, I'll have you know that, for my part, I am enthralled with my Emily just the way she is.

LORD LOVEWORTHY: I am pleased to hear it.

EARL: And at the moment, she is a woman desirous of a tattoo. And I wouldn't have her any other way.

LORD LOVEWORTHY: Well, I will have her the way God and her mother intended her: Pure, pristine and unblemished. As a virgin snowfall on an unspoiled landscape, surrounding an equally virginal lake, whose untrammeled shores have never felt the taint of man!

EMILY: Oh, this is pure prudery. The only vices you like in a young lady are excessive love of cooking, and the cleaning of kitchenware.

LORD LOVEWORTHY: And an affection for her parents that borders on the Oedipal.

LADY LILLIAN: She may also do needlepoint.

EMILY: Oh...oh... Frippery!

LADY LILLIAN: Emily! Your language!

EMILY: Frippery! Frippery!

LADY LILLIAN: Fennimore! Fetch soap.

LORD LOVEWORTHY: Well, this certainly settles the matter, Mister Kant. I am sorry. You seem like a decent sort, though scruffy. And for a brief moment I had even entertained the notion of allowing you to marry into our family after all.

LADY LILLIAN: We have a spinster niece with only somewhat of a hunch.

LORD LOVEWORTHY: But these latest revelations are simply too shocking. I could never entrust the welfare of my relations, however distant and repulsive, to the

care of a man who would allow them to further
disfeature themselves in so scandalous a manner.

EMILY: Father, you have yet to hear the most scandalous
thing of all.

LORD LOVEWORTHY: What is that?

MILES: Millicent, cover your eyes.

EMILY: Earl owns a bookery.

LORD LOVEWORTHY: A what?

EMILY: Among his many enterprises is a quaint little
book shop tucked away in the alley behind the tattoo
parlour.

MILES: Ha ha! A book shop? Is it possible, Sir Cyril?
You and this degenerate bugbear may have a common
interest. Lord Loveworthy is a novelist, you know.
Perhaps you have sold some of his books.

EARL: Oh, that's not likely.

MILES: Of course, it is. He is a celebrated author. His
first novel is still regarded in academic circles as one
of the finest works in the English language.

EARL: I'm sure it is, but if that's the case, my customers
wouldn't care for it. They're not much for fine English.
No offense, sir.

MILES: Ah, the American flair for bigotry rears its
patriotic head. So they won't read a book if it's English?

EARL: No, they won't read it if it's fine. I specialize in
books of a more venial vein.

MILES: I'm sure modesty prevents his Lordship from
pointing out that his *Memoirs of a Parisian Tourist* is
altogether gripping. Have you read it?

EARL: No, sir, I am not well-read.

EMILY: In fact, he is illiterate.

MILES: Then how can you possibly manage a book shop?

EARL: I only judge a book by its pictures.

MILES: What sort of book is sold on the strength of its illustrations?

EARL: Erotic fiction, of course.

EMILY: Earl is a pornographer!

(MILES, MILLICENT, LORD LOVEWORTHY *and* LADY LILLIAN *stand in stunned silence.*)

FENNIMORE: Oh... *(He faints!)*

END OF ACT TWO

ACT THREE
A Series of Shocking Revelations

(Scene: The parlour of Loveworthy Manor.)

LORD LOVEWORTHY: Fennimore! You fainted.

FENNIMORE: Yes, sir.

LORD LOVEWORTHY: Whatever for?

FENNIMORE: I thought the moment warranted it, sir. And as no one else seemed likely to oblige, I took it upon myself. I hope I have not overstepped.

LORD LOVEWORTHY: I appreciate the initiative, Fennimore, but it was utterly unnecessary. Her Ladyship and I are quite capable of falling into our own swoons as the need arises.

FENNIMORE: The world's a stage, sir: One mustn't miss one's cue to be dramatic.

LORD LOVEWORTHY: You might at least have set down your serving tray before you undertook the role. Now her Ladyship shall have to clean up after you. Lillian, look at this mess.

LADY LILLIAN: You needn't nag, I have the matter well in hand. Fennimore!

FENNIMORE: Yes, milady?

LADY LILLIAN: See to this at once.

(FENNIMORE *produces a rag and soap, and begins cleaning up.)*

LORD LOVEWORTHY: And in future, please allow Lady Lillian and myself to register appropriate shock on behalf of the household.

MILES: But, Sir Cyril, you don't seem to be registering anything of the sort, appropriate or otherwise. Your daughter has just exposed her fiancé for not only an avowed American, but a profligate pornographer as well. Is no one else scandalized by this?

LADY LILLIAN: You seem to be scandalized enough for the whole parlour.

MILES: This is no smirking matter, Lady Lillian. We are in the presence of an unrepentant, erotic entrepreneur who has designs upon your unmarried, yet marriageable daughter. Do neither of you perceive the inherent peril in indifference to this predicament? Or are Millicent and I the only ones who have not lost all sense of moral perspective?

MILLICENT: Speak for yourself, Miles. I, for one, find the Earl quite charming in despite of his outward scruff and his presumably low birth.

EARL: Much obliged.

LORD LOVEWORTHY: Perspective, it seems, is also in the eye of the beholder.

MILLICENT: And where, may I ask, is the harm in a bit of innocuous erotica? Why, the novel I'm reading at the moment is a naughty French trifle called *Dame Chelsea's Complaint*, and I am none the worse for it.

EARL: Actually, it's Italian. Or Belgian, I think. One of our best sellers. The first in a series, in fact. Very popular with the ladies. And seagoing gents.

LADY LILLIAN: Does its action unfold on the high seas?

EARL: No, but theirs does. And one likes a good book after.

EMILY: It is the tale of the chaste Chelsea Cherryweather of Chatsworth, who enters the story a supple, virgin bride and leaves it a woman tragically fulfilled.

MILLICENT: Miss Emily! Are you familiar with *Dame Chelsea's Complaint*, as well?

EMILY: It's how Earl and I met. As I trekked across the American continent on my journey of self-discovery, I found myself in Arizona, alone and feeling homesick. So I stopped into Earl's book shop for the smell of the bindings. It always reminds me of Father's study and home.

EARL: I caught her sniffing the fiction and offered to recommend a book she might find sufficiently visceral.

EMILY: He gave me *Dame Chelsea's Complaint*, and I devoured it cover-to-cover on the spot, and returned the next morning for more.

MILES: Aha! I know your ilk, Mister Kant. A susceptible young innocent chances into your clutches and your first thought is to seduce her with this corruption. Perhaps that is the American way, but in England it is a punishable offense. Why, just last Thursday, the *Times* reported the case of a sequestered invert who lured young monastic students to their decay with borrowed copies of Darwin's treatises. He was arrested forthwith and hanged as an evolutionist.

MILLICENT: *Dame Chelsea's Complaint* is hardly heretical. I daresay the timely application of an occasional romantic novella now and again has done more to preserve the sanctity and longevity of our happy marriage than your belated boxes of anniversary chocolates.

LADY LILLIAN: Mrs Monger, you make this licentiousness seem almost medicinal.

MILLICENT: I suppose it can be, Lady Lillian. When Miles and I are on a tiff, or he's become remote and distant, lost in his work again, I find it invigorating to become lost myself in a good fiction. I like to imagine myself in the shoes of Lady Chelsea. And in her petticoats.

EMILY: She also has a very nice collection of hats.

MILLICENT: Naturally, I imagine my husband Miles in the role of the rakish blackmailer.

MILES: Rakish blackmailer? In my entire life, I have never been rakish with so much as a leaf-strewn lawn.

MILLICENT: More's the pity. The lawn could use it.

LADY LILLIAN: You mustn't take it personally, Miles. A woman's fantasies are not meant to be plausible. That would be a waste of good imagination.

MILLICENT: It is a momentary escape that leaves me exhilarated and capable of coping with his withering distempers.

LADY LILLIAN: Well, I have never partaken of this particular perversity, but one does not need a surgical degree to appreciate the appeal of the penchant.

EMILY: Mother! In all my childhood, I would not have taken you for such a freethinker.

LADY LILLIAN: Well, you are old enough now to know that I am your mother, not a corpse.

MILES: Lord Loveworthy, are you going to say nothing about this?

LORD LOVEWORTHY: About what? It appears that women are wont to want what they will, and there is nothing for it but to give them precisely that or stand out of the way while they get it themselves. There is no evading the dictates of one's destiny, or one's gender.

MILES: Indeed, if I've learned nothing today, it is that the weaker sex can be quite strong-willed in their frailties. Nonetheless, sir, you are a public figure of some small renown. I should think you would be concerned for your reputation having works of obscenity discussed so openly in your own parlour. Why, if any of my colleagues at the *Times* discovered you were party to this bawdy debate, which I assure you they shall not for my presence here implicates me in this indecence as well, it would be an end to your reputation there.

LADY LILLIAN: Or the beginning of a colorful new one.

LORD LOVEWORTHY: Her Ladyship posits a compelling point, Miles. How do you suppose it would impact my reputation at the *Times* if it were thought that I, too, were an erotic epicure?

MILES: You, sir? You would dare to indulge in this feminine drivel?

EARL: How would you know it's drivel, without having read it yourself?

MILES: I'll have you know, I am a respected literary critic. I don't need to subject myself to obscenity to know it for what it is, sight unseen. And I should hope that Lord Loveworthy could say the same. To think: Sir Cyril, a reader of rank erotica. At least assure me you are not avid.

LORD LOVEWORTHY: There's no need to fret on that account, for I am neither avid, nor a reader of pornography.

MILES: That is a considerable relief.

LORD LOVEWORTHY: On the contrary, I write it.

LADY LILLIAN: Write it? You? Ha! (*Catching herself*) Excuse me.

LORD LOVEWORTHY: Gesundheit, my dear. But your darkly satiric allergies, notwithstanding, I have become quite adept at it and rather successful in the field. The publication of pornography has, in fact, become something of a second profession.

MILES: Why, this is unheard of!

EARL: No, offense, sir, but if you were any good at it, I would have heard of you.

LORD LOVEWORTHY: It is precisely because it is unheard of that you have not, for decorum has forced me to pen my earthier works under an assumed pseudonym.

MILLICENT: An erotic nom de plume. How novel!

EARL: It's quite common, actually. Many of the finest pornographers resort to anonymity to spare their families the humiliation of widespread success and celebrity. Miriam Merrymount. Bonnie Mae Blowell. Father Shamus Bollix. None of these are genuine identities. And you, sir? What do you call yourself?

LORD LOVEWORTHY: I go by the name Cherryweather. Chelsea Cherryweather.

MILLICENT: Oh! Oh my!

LORD LOVEWORTHY: And she's British.

MILLICENT: Chelsea Cherryweather! Here, in person! And in the person of our own Lord Loveworthy. Oh, Miles, I don't know whether to cry or blush or faint or sit down and catch my breath.

MILES: Well, I know what you should be doing, and it's none of the former, for we all ought to be quivering with outrage. Outrage, Sir Cyril!

LORD LOVEWORTHY: I heard you the first time, Miles.

MILES: It bore repeating. Outrage! There, I've said it thrice.

MILLICENT: Oh, be quiet, Miles. You, Sir Cyril, are my hero. And my heroine. I have always been an admirer of your work, but now, Sir Cyril... I am an admirer of your work.

LORD LOVEWORTHY: Mrs Monger, I am flattered by the implication of your inflection. But you are a married woman. As am I. Married, that is.

MILLICENT: *(Blushing)* Oh, I hope you have not taken my impassioned adulation for crass infatuation, for I mean nothing forward or untoward by it. Although I must admit, if honesty be permitted, that your latest creation elicits such illicit elations as I have never hitherto encountered, except in the still quietude of nature. Or a vigorous horseback ride.

MILES: This is an outrage!

LADY LILLIAN: You have said as much, Miles. May we move on to a fresher expression?

MILES: Mrs Loveworthy, I am astounded that you are not more openly horrified.

LADY LILLIAN: I suppose I would be, were I not utterly disinterested in my husband's literary escapades. But as I have neither read, nor cared to read, any of his prior works, I don't see how the experience of not reading this new one shall substantially differ.

MILES: Your husband is a novelist. How can you not have read his books?

LADY LILLIAN: By letting them lie unopened on the shelf.

MILES: But it is how he makes his living. And yours!

LADY LILLIAN: And so long as he continues to do so,
I remain content to leave him to it, and not take issue
with his methods.

LORD LOVEWORTHY: In her steadfast indifference, Lady
Lillian has always been staunchly insupportive of my
career.

LADY LILLIAN: It's the very least I could do. In truth,
I find my husband's writing, on the whole, tedious,
having had to endure many interminable evenings of
poetic discourse in the course of our courtship. It was
during a recitation of a sonnet on his fondness for the
Industrial Revolution, inasmuch as its technological
upheavals brought to mind the heaving of my bosom,
that I learned to loathe his eloquence.

LORD LOVEWORTHY: You would have preferred a
limerick?

LADY LILLIAN: Ah, that boundless wit. Would we could
bottle it! Or cage it. Or toss it down a well.

MILES: Whether or not his talent is to your taste, it is
human nature to care what he has done with it. Why,
I have made a career of forming opinions on things that
did not directly concern me.

LADY LILLIAN: Whereas, I, on the other hand, have
never concerned myself whether a tree fallen in the
woods made a sound, so long as I was not there to hear
it.

MILES: Well, then perhaps you should hear what your
husband has been doing in the woods!

(MILES *snatches the novel out of* MILLICENT's *hand and
reads it aloud.*)

LORD LOVEWORTHY: Miles, no—

MILES: Chapter the third! "The whole of my being
trembled in anticipation of his marauding caress,

a quickening in my blood which heralded a dawning of
a new desire. A feral urge which only feral means could
sate. Our bated breaths hung in the chill night air in
tiny tufts of temptatious exhalations, as his inquisitive
fingers probed for answers only my modesty could
provide. Until at last, I felt the first rude intrusion of
a husband's touch, though not from husband's hand.
An unaccustomed intimacy. A strange familiarity.
An alien invasion."

LADY LILLIAN: Stop!

MILLICENT: No, don't stop!

EMILY: Not just yet!

LADY LILLIAN: I said, enough!

MILES: There! Do not you recoil in horror, or some other
attitude of aversion? Are you not sickened to the very
quick?

LADY LILLIAN: I am quite beyond sickness and recoil at
what you have just read, for it is without question the
most heinous betrayal of marital troth I have ever
heard, seen, imagined, or dreamt in my vilest
nightmares.

LORD LOVEWORTHY: And for that, dear, I sincerely
apologize.

MILLICENT: You mustn't be cross with him, Lady
Lillian. It is only a fiction, after all, and the whole genre
is prone to prurience. And honestly, Miles, one mustn't
leap into the midst of a story like that. I'm sure the
exposition makes clear that Dame Chelsea succumbed
to wanton lustfulness only out of spite for a loveless
marriage, or as a result of financial circumstance.
Or the vapours.

LORD LOVEWORTHY: I'm afraid, Mrs Monger, that her Ladyship is not offended at Chelsea Cherryweather's betrayal.

MILLICENT: She's not?

LADY LILLIAN: I'm offended at his!

(LADY LILLIAN *points at* LORD LOVEWORTHY.)

MILES: And well you should be. For his behavior effects your standing in the community as much as it does his own. Why, concern for your good name alone should have prevailed upon him to eschew such pornographic pursuits. To scorn all propriety and embarrass one's spouse, and by association one's neighbors, in so flagrant a fashion is unfathomable. I am quite beyond speech.

LORD LOVEWORTHY: Then you will be positively silent with rage to learn that the transgression is far worse than you imagine.

MILES: Worse? What could be worse than the loss of one's reputation?

LORD LOVEWORTHY: The gain of one, of course.

MILES: What do you mean by that?

LADY LILLIAN: What you have just read aloud for all to hear, and Lord Loveworthy has published abroad for the world to read, is an indecent passage stolen verbatim from my personal and private diary.

MILLICENT: Oh my.

EMILY: Oh, Mother.

EARL: Oh, brother.

MILES: Do you mean to say that, in your own journals, you refer to yourself as Dame Chelsea Cherryweather, the chaste maid of Chatsworth?

LORD LOVEWORTHY: No, that particular alliteration is an editorial elision on my part, to protect the identities of those innocent. But everything else in it is a direct transcript.

MILES: Egad! Sir Cyril, a plagiarist?! This is an ethical abuse of the highest breach. To pass oneself off as a reputed fictionalist, only to be found in the end, no more than a rank copyist.

MILLICENT: Oh, Miles... Shut up.

(MILES *notices* LADY LILLIAN *glaring at* LORD LOVEWORTHY *and realizes he should let her go first.*)

MILES: But we can talk about that later.

LADY LILLIAN: How could you, Cyril? My innermost secrets dashed across the pages of inexpensive and tawdry publications and sold to all comers at newsstands and bawdy establishments.

LORD LOVEWORTHY: If it is any consolation, the illustrations are quite tasteful.

LADY LILLIAN: Cyril... I do not think that I shall ever have cause to forgive you for this.

MILES: Nor should you. A lady's privacy should be foremost in her husband's protection: Inviolate even to the prying eyes of those closest to her. Especially himself! Lady Lillian, my wife Millicent and I stand beside you in your affrontment, and if we may be of any solace or sanctuary in this, your hour of direst duress, or should you need a bed and comfort in your impending and inevitable separation pursuant to divorce, the door to our guest house is always open to you. Isn't that right, dear?

MILLICENT: *(Bitterly)* I think she's had bed and comfort enough.

MILES: Millicent! Surely it is our Christian duty to offer refuge to the wife of a man accused of making a mockery of their marriage in the parlour over tea.

MILLICENT: It was not in the parlour that a mockery was made of this marriage.

MILES: What is that supposed to mean?

EMILY: It has been some time since I read *Dame Chelsea's Complaint,* but if memory serves: Does not the chaste young Chelsea first make a mockery of her marital vows in the nave, with the rakish gardener?

MILLICENT: No, it is in the garden that she makes a mockery of her marriage. ...With the rakish neighbor.

MILES: What?! I—! *(To* LADY LILLIAN*)* You put that in your diary?! *(To the others)* And if she did, it is a deplorable lie, and I am appalled.

LORD LOVEWORTHY: If she lies, she does so quite elaborately, and in explicit detail throughout chapters two through six of my book: Lady Chelsea, barely returned from her honeymoon, and strolling alone in the garden, unexpectedly comes upon and subsequently succumbs to the passions of the rakish neighbor, Deacon Derek Dildover.

MILES: Dildover?!

LORD LOVEWORTHY: Yes, Dildover!

MILES: I think I resent the sound of that.

LORD LOVEWORTHY: And I resent that you have plundered my marital bed!

MILES: I am no plunderer!

LADY LILLIAN: And I am no man's plunder!

LORD LOVEWORTHY: Oh, there's no question that you were a willing participant in your beplunderment. But

it is plunder nonetheless. I can think of no other term
for it.

EMILY: Sensual seduction?

MILLICENT: Savage enravagement?

FENNIMORE: Salacious relations? Libidinous diddling?

LORD LOVEWORTHY: I stand corrected.

FENNIMORE: Bodily dawdling? Coital loitering?

LORD LOVEWORTHY: There are any number of evocative
euphemisms—

FENNIMORE: Rotterdam and thank you, ma'am?

LORD LOVEWORTHY: But there is no mistaking their
literal meaning. For the very definition is spelled
out here in my book, in its every lurid nuance.

LADY LILLIAN: I'm sure that it is. You were always
meticulous even in your tedium.

EMILY: Mother, how could you?

LADY LILLIAN: I admit that I may have strayed on
occasion from my nuptial obligations.

LORD LOVEWORTHY: And those occasions appear to be
weekends, Tuesdays and national holidays.

LADY LILLIAN: But does your torrid little tell-all dare to
delineate Dame Chelsea's reasons for taking up with
the roguish gardener?

EMILY: Rakish.

EARL: Neighbor.

LORD LOVEWORTHY: Deacon, actually.

LADY LILLIAN: Does it say that she strayed from the
holy vows which she held to be inviolable only because
you first strayed from yours.

EMILY: Mother! ...Father?

LADY LILLIAN: With her! *(She points at* MILLICENT.*)*

EMILY: Mrs Monger?!

MILLICENT: I—? Oh! Oh no! Oh! Oh, Miles. I— Oh...
(She runs out of the room.)

LADY LILLIAN: There's a guilty swoon if I ever saw one!

LORD LOVEWORTHY: Lillian, how did you discover the
affair betwixt Mrs. Monger and myself? Who told you?

LADY LILLIAN: Who told me? Then you don't even
bother to deny it? He did, of course. *(She points at*
MILES.*)*

LORD LOVEWORTHY: Miles?

EMILY: Yes, Father, as it clearly states in your book.
Deacon Dildover, returning early one Sunday from
church business, discovered yourself and his wife
frolicking in his bedchambers as one should only frolic
in one's own bedchambers, with one's own spouse.
Or a beagle pup. Inconsolable with grief, he rushed
across the neighboring lawn to the only soul in whom
he could confide his shame: my mother. Finding her
alone in the garden, he revealed to her the sinful
explicitnesses he had just witnessed and, in a fit of
punitive passion, she succumbed to his suggestion
of reciprocal fornication.

LADY LILLIAN: Don't look at me like that. Do you
think I would have given myself over to a disagreeable,
sordid little man like Miles Monger if he hadn't been
the only one here to console me when I learned that
you had betrayed me, and his wife him, with you?

MILES: I am not little.

LADY LILLIAN: But I did not do it out of mere lust,
or passion, or even consolement. I seized the moment
to be dramatic. For I was unfaithful to you with the

husband of the very woman with whom you had been unfaithful to me. Millicent Monger!

LORD LOVEWORTHY: I see. And in chapter seven, when you required further consolation.

EMILY: Father, enough!

LORD LOVEWORTHY: Emily, I know it must be difficult for you: Seeing your parents in all their human frailties—

EMILY: I am not so sheltered from the world of parental frailty as you might have yourself believe. I have read at least one book on the subject, after all.

EARL: Emily—

EMILY: Not now, Earl. I make no excuses for my mother. What she did was lewd, despicable, and very well-written.

LADY LILLIAN: Thank you.

EMILY: But she did it out of vengeance, not lechery.

LORD LOVEWORTHY: And you think that excuses her?

EMILY: No, but it does beg the question...

LORD LOVEWORTHY: Yes?

EMILY: What's your excuse?

LORD LOVEWORTHY: For what?

EMILY: For seducing Millicent Monger!

LORD LOVEWORTHY: Oh, didn't I tell you—?

(LORD LOVEWORTHY *is interrupted by the sound of a gunshot in the garden!*)

MILES: What was that?

LORD LOVEWORTHY: The stinging ring of a single gunshot!

(...Followed by a heavy thud)

EARL: And the heavy thump of a body slumping to the ground.

MILES: Millicent!

(Strangely, no one reacts. They all just stand there, rather numbly.)

(With a sigh of resignation, FENNIMORE sets down his tray, and prepares to faint. LORD LOVEWORTHY stops him.)

LORD LOVEWORTHY: That won't be necessary.

(FENNIMORE refrains from fainting. He picks up his tray and exits.)

END OF ACT THREE

ACT FOUR
Horrible, Beastly People

(Scene: The parlour of Loveworthy Manor)

LORD LOVEWORTHY: I suppose now it falls to one of us to discover the body.

MILES: Well, it is your house.

LORD LOVEWORTHY: And she is your wife.

MILES: That hardly seems relevant to the question of jurisdiction.

LORD LOVEWORTHY: Perhaps not. But as a matter of courtesy, it would be impolite of me to begrudge you the exercise of your full marital rights.

MILES: Marital rights? What exactly do you imagine I should do with her? Though I don't suppose I care to know where a pornographer's flights of fancy have taken him.

LORD LOVEWORTHY: I mean only that you might wish to discover the body yourself, that you may take a moment alone to mourn in privacy.

MILES: I would not want to snoop about your premises.

LORD LOVEWORTHY: Your respect for my premises is appreciated. If belated.

LADY LILLIAN: If I am to be regarded as anyone's premises, I should like it to be my own.

LORD LOVEWORTHY: As you have demonstrated by making yourself everyone else's, but I am referring to the house. You see, Miles has been surreptitiously coming and going from this estate at his will and leisure for almost as long as we have known him.

MILES: There is no proof of that!

LORD LOVEWORTHY: As Dame Chelsea reports repeatedly in her diaries.

MILES: Other than the published accounts.

LORD LOVEWORTHY: The reader is tempted to infer that the fictional Lady Chelsea might have resisted the good deacon's further temptations had he not so conveniently appeared to her in all her hours of distress, and various states of undress. But after their initial assignation in the garden, he again encounters her alone and unannounced in the parlour, the pantry, the privy—

MILES: I took a wrong turn.

LORD LOVEWORTHY: Always, of course, to Dame Chelsea's mystification—

LADY LILLIAN: It did seem quite a coincidence, now you mention it.

LORD LOVEWORTHY: Though even a cursory reader can come to the clarion conclusion...

EARL & EMILY: He has a key.

LADY LILLIAN: He what?

LORD LOVEWORTHY: When you served in the Infantry, Miles, were you not so petrified at the sound of Gatling-fire that you requested assignment to the corps of homeland engineers, where you specialized as a gunnery locksmith?

MILES: If you are implying that I am any less a patriot for having served my tour of duty helping our fighting men gain access to their footlockers, then you are not overly familiar with the contents of a footlocker.

LORD LOVEWORTHY: I am implying only that your new-found respect for my domestic boundaries seems, at best, hyperbolic, given that you made yourself a key.

LADY LILLIAN: You have a key? Then those were not chance encounters in the garden, the pantry, the master bath? We were not hurled repeatedly into each other's arms by the fickle finger of Fate?

LORD LOVEWORTHY: No, my dear. I'm afraid the fickle hurler was Premeditated Lust. And I don't think that was his finger.

MILES: Were I not, presently, in mourning, I should take exception to your intimation.

LORD LOVEWORTHY: It is premature to be in mourning for someone who has not as yet been determined to be deceased. Now, will you go and see for yourself what has become of Mrs Monger or do you persist in insisting that I, as your host, attend to the matter?

MILES: Neither, Sir Cyril, for given the circumstances, the responsibility should fall, naturally, to Mrs Loveworthy.

LADY LILLIAN: To me?

MILES: You are, after all, the Lady of the Manor. And therefore, a woman.

LADY LILLIAN: And when did undertaking become a wifely undertaking?

MILES: Six weeks ago Friday. Or do neither of you read the papers?

LORD LOVEWORTHY: Indeed I do! Aloud at breakfast.

LADY LILLIAN: He is tedious in many things.

LORD LOVEWORTHY: You must admit it has kept you abreast of events.

LADY LILLIAN: You are edifying, if nothing else. Which is generally the case.

MILES: Then you both no doubt recall the recent sensational and unseemly story of the Duchess of Devonsfordshire, recounted in the *Times* three fortnights ago.

LORD LOVEWORTHY: The unfortunate widow who died penniless, intoxicated and nude in the backroom of a Beddington brothel?

MILES: That is she. It seems that the good Duchess's late Duke had acquired gambling debts which, upon his passing, she could only honour by dishonouring herself and two of her three under-age children in a burlesque act of dubious taste and legality. Ultimately, the shame of it was more than she could bear. Seized with a fit of hysteric depression, and with the gaming authorities closing in, she chose to end her life in a fashion both poetic and pathetic.

LADY LILLIAN: I remember this story: The inspectors discovered her body, poised like a Renaissance nude, reclining upon a bed of rose petals, with a single lit candle in one hand and all her remaining modesty in the other, having succumbed to a fatal excess of absinthe and cooking sherry. Her suicide has been the talk of all the more fashionable gossip circles since.

MILES: The Duchess having popularized the genre, the authorities fear that we are bound to see an outbreak of similar self-humiliations among women of status. And on the chance that Millicent, in her present distraction, has emulated the Duchess's example, it would be unbecoming of either Lord Loveworthy or myself to be the first to come upon her in such a state of feminine disarray.

LORD LOVEWORTHY: Do you really think it likely that your wife has fled to the garden and, in distress, disrobed and disposed of herself?

MILES: What I consider likely is hardly the best barometer for what has precipitated here today.

EMILY: Unpredictability *has* been the order of the afternoon.

MILES: Why, for all we know, it is not my wife who is lying dead and disheveled in your garden, but your butler Fennimore, fully clothed and in the foyer. Or trussed like a pig in the pantry.

LADY LILLIAN: What a ghastly speculation! If it is Fennimore, we must contact the papers immediately!

MILES: Would not Scotland Yard be better suited to the task?

LADY LILLIAN: Of hiring a new butler? The matter is urgent, but hardly criminal. I'm sure the classifieds will satisfy.

LORD LOVEWORTHY: You are right, my dear, we must place an advertisement at once. The finest help is hardest found.

LADY LILLIAN: Fennimore!

(Enter FENNIMORE with a paper and pen.)

FENNIMORE: Yes, milady?

LADY LILLIAN: Send a cable at once: Manservant wanted. Stop.

LORD LOVEWORTHY: Lillian dear, stop.

LADY LILLIAN: Oh. There you are.

LORD LOVEWORTHY: Well, that rules out Fennimore.

MILES: Yes, well... The point being: Who can say what mad behaviors may have seized my Millicent in her self-destructive dysphoria?

LORD LOVEWORTHY: Well, in any case, we will not know exactly what has or has not happened and to whom until one or more of us takes it upon him or herself to search the house. Or at least the garden. And they should do so at once without further delay!

(They do nothing.)

MILES: Shall we draw lots for it, then?

LADY LILLIAN: If we are drawing lots, I must insist that Emily be exempt, she is too young. And we have raised her not to gamble.

LORD LOVEWORTHY: And Earl Kant, of course, cannot, as he is our guest.

MILES: I am your guest as well, or had you forgotten?

LORD LOVEWORTHY: But she is your wife. Surely, that status supersedes your guesthood.

MILES: Then I must additionally abstain on grounds of gambling, for you know it is a vice in which I, too, do not indulge.

LORD LOVEWORTHY: One would wish that hypocrisy were a habit from which you could likewise refrain.

MILES: Hypocrisy?!

LORD LOVEWORTHY: Yes, and cowardice! For it is not the threat of artillery fire that keeps you from the forefront in this bloody instance, but your own unseemly and unmanly squeamishness.

MILES: Oh! And you, sir, are a cuckold. Your lady a slattern. And your daughter is fat!

EMILY: Oh!

LORD LOVEWORTHY: I say!

LADY LILLIAN: Well!

EARL: Now, see here!

LORD LOVEWORTHY: Mister Monger, I will tolerate no more of your reckless disparagements on my premises. Fennimore! Fetch me a glove.

MILES: I would like one as well, Fennimore.

LORD LOVEWORTHY: A pair of gloves, Fennimore!

(FENNIMORE *returns with a pair of gloves on a tray.*)

FENNIMORE: Ahem... Leather gloves! A pair! Opera-length!

LORD LOVEWORTHY: These are ladies gloves, Fennimore.

FENNIMORE: Thought you might find that insulting, sir.

LORD LOVEWORTHY: I do! Well, done, Fennimore!

(LORD LOVEWORTHY *takes up one, and* MILES *the other.*)

LORD LOVEWORTHY: Mister Monger, if you do not at once search this house for the earthly remains of your dear wife, I shall brutally slap you.

MILES: And I, you, if you do not the same, out of hospitality.

LORD LOVEWORTHY: Very well, then. Slap on!

MILES: After you.

LORD LOVEWORTHY: Be my guest.

MILES: I am your guest.

EMILY: Oh, I will do it! (*She snatches the gloves and slaps them both.*) You are all such horrible, beastly people! I thought, coming here today, having returned from America, with a string of fresh vices, a poor choice of husband, and an ill-considered tattoo, that I, for once, would be the talk of the tea, and not this perpetual

peevishness. But I see now that one may travel the
world in search of depravity and never find so much
of it as lies heaped in one's own back yard. Or in the
garden. You are all abhorrently boorish and whorish
and rude, and were I not related to some of you,
I should love nothing more than to have nothing
more to do with you for so long as I live. But as we
are not entirely unrelated: Father, I shall expect you at
my impending wedding, to give me away with your
blessing. And Mother to weep. And thereafter I shall
endeavor never to speak to either of you ever again.
Mister Monger, it has been a pleasure to meet you
and your lovely wife, and a horrible embarrassment.
And my condolences. Earl, come with me. We are
going to move a body. Again!

(EMILY *exits into the garden.*)

EARL: She's right, you know. If you don't mind my
saying.

LORD LOVEWORTHY: Speak freely, Mister Kant, for you
are very soon to be family, and lose that luxury once
and for all.

EARL: I know it's not my place, as a guest in this house,
and a foreigner in this land—and as an American—
to judge the likes of you. But I think I can judge my
Emily, and I tell you this: She is as kind and caring
a soul as any I've known. And I know quite a few
sheepdogs. And she's as strong and spirited as any
man and his horse. But kindness and strength are
fragile attributes. It takes but a bit of bitterness to
turn them both to vinegar and piss. Emily aspires to
your disapproval, because that is how she was raised.
But she deserves to have been sprung from better roots.
And if my crude exterior can shield her from so refined
a fate as has befallen the lot of you, I will consider
I have served her better than any haughty Earl ever
could.

LORD LOVEWORTHY: And serve you shall. Thank you.
And congratulations, Mister Kant.

(EARL *exits*.)

LADY LILLIAN: Well, that's that. My nerves are quite
frayed, and the aforementioned depravity having
thoroughly exhausted me, I shall retire to my
bed-quarters. I suspect I shall have quite a novel
to write tonight.

LORD LOVEWORTHY: Before you go, dear, did you not
desire the answer to your question?

LADY LILLIAN: Which question?

LORD LOVEWORTHY: As to whether my novel reveals
that Dame Chelsea was driven to her initial infidelity
by the news of her husband's.

LADY LILLIAN: I don't suppose it matters, now that
your poor depraved mistress is lying dead among the
philodendrons. Whether the story is accurate and you
are an adulterer, or abridged and you are a perjurer,
is immaterial to the fact that you are either one or the
other and neither one pleasant.

LORD LOVEWORTHY: I see. Then it will not interest
you to know that every word of Deacon Dildover's
portrayal of Lord Cherryweather's betrayal is contained
in *Dame Chelsea's Complaint*. The book is scrupulously
faithful to its source.

LADY LILLIAN: Well, that's one of you. Good night.

LORD LOVEWORTHY: What the book does not say is that
Dame Chelsea's source is faithful to nothing, for he is
an unscrupulous liar.

MILES: How dare you!

LORD LOVEWORTHY: I said it does not say it. The book is
defending you on this point.

MILES: It would be slander if it did not, for I am nothing if not honest.

LORD LOVEWORTHY: Then you are honestly somewhat less than nothing.

MILES: Oh!

LORD LOVEWORTHY: You see, my dear Lillian, the novel, like your diary, is told entirely from the protagonist's point of view, therefore it cannot know anything she does not, to wit: that the rakish blackmailer fabricated a fictional affair with his wife, in order to engage you in a genuine affair with himself, under false pretenses.

LADY LILLIAN: You don't mean...?

LORD LOVEWORTHY: Lillian, by all that I hold holy, dear and tasteful, I have never—nor would I ever—nor could I ever, frankly, now that she is deceased—take up with Mrs Monger. Such a carnal betrayal goes against my very grain, and the solemn vows we both have sworn. Nor do I believe that you would have forsaken yours had you not believed in good faith that I had already done so, with mine, in bad.

LADY LILLIAN: No, I wouldn't. Oh, Cyril! What have I done?

LORD LOVEWORTHY: As for the reason Miles chose to break his own sacred oaths in direct defiance of church, state and etiquette, I can only surmise. Perhaps it was covetousness that I had an opulent home, where his was modest, a vivacious wife, where his was plain, a promising career, where he was a failed writer. ...But he knew how to get the wife.

MILES: I am not a failed writer! I am a successful critic!!

LORD LOVEWORTHY: Are not the two synonymous?

LADY LILLIAN: Miles, is this true? Millicent never betrayed you?

MILES: Yes, she did! He knows she did! Lord Loveworthy may feign his disdain, but she was unfaithful to me in a manner so hideous and unforgivable that only another writer could understand, for she loved his words better than mine!

LADY LILLIAN: Ah.

MILES: It was not always so. When first we wed she used to hang upon every inkling from my pen. One quip of my critiques spoke more for her than a thousand pages of whatever dreck I was condemning. But in the end, it was my own brilliance and the blissfulness of our happy home, which were my undoing. For I became too soft in my criticism, and too clever in my praise. When I commended Lord Loveworthy's first novel with all the heartfelt joy that comes of marital contentment, my wife became so smitten with my robust and glowing opinion that she insisted on reading the subject matter itself. I tried to discourage her, but I had lost her to my own superlative powers of persuasion. She soon became an admirer of Lord Loveworthy's work and of every tedious word he eked upon a page.

LORD LOVEWORTHY: I am sorry, Miles.

MILES: Imagine then, my chagrin when the two of you moved into the adjoining estate. You, the man whose wit she loved more than mine. And you, the woman whose bosom heaves like a thousand hydraulic printing presses!

LADY LILLIAN: Oh.

LORD LOVEWORTHY: Mind your metaphors, Miles.

MILES: From the moment we became neighbors, my wife could not stop thinking about him. His words

were ever on her lips. His ideas in her head. What
mattered if her mere body was true to my marriage
bed? Her thoughts were over here, night after night,
dallying with yours. Wallowing in sheets of his prose.
Lying in sin with his imagery. Like a literary strumpet.
An intellectual harlot. A bibliophiliac whore!

(Enter MILLICENT, *still very much alive, with* FENNIMORE,
EMILY *and* EARL.*)*

FENNIMORE: Ahem... This way, Mrs Monger. Steady.
Mind your step.

MILLICENT: Thank you, Fennimore. I am feeling much
better now.

LORD LOVEWORTHY: Better? Mrs Monger, you are
positively perambulatory!

MILES: But how? We heard the gunshot.

LADY LILLIAN: And the sickening thud.

MILLICENT: *(Horribly embarrassed)* Oh, that. Yes, I ran
into the garden, distraught, as you can imagine, having
been accused of an adulterous act which I could not
have imagined committing with anyone save my
husband—whose own commitment, it seems, was not
mutual—and finding Sir Cyril's grandfather's pistols
lying where Lady Lillian and I had left them, decided
then and there to do mischief upon myself and my
marriage. As is the fashion, you may have heard.

LADY LILLIAN: Yes, yes, we completely understand.
Except the men.

MILLICENT: I had, however, the presence of mind to
first fire a trial round into the delphiniums to see if
I knew how to operate the accursed instrument of my
intended destruction. The noise was so loud, and the
damage to your flower beds—I'm sorry, Fennimore—
so horrific, that I fainted dead away at the sight.

FENNIMORE: Hence, the gunfire, and the sickening thud.

LORD LOVEWORTHY: Yes, Fennimore, we are following the narrative.

MILLICENT: When I came to, determined still to make an end of myself, I soon surmised that the attempt would be in vain, for I knew not how to reload.

MILES: There are two pistols, Millicent. You might have used the other one.

(MILLICENT *glowers at* MILES.)

MILLICENT: Yes, but the second bullet was intended for you. And there was no point in killing my husband next, if I could not first finish myself.

MILES: Oh.

MILLICENT: But since you don't like to see things go to waste, Miles, I'll be happy to have Fennimore fetch the other pistol in for you.

MILES: Thank you, no, you made a wise choice letting us live.

MILLICENT: Yes, now that I've had a moment's ponderance, I recognize that suicide is far too gruesome a fate for me, and too succinct a one for you.

MILES: I beg your pardon?

MILLICENT: Lord and Lady Loveworthy, I apologize if I or my husband have created an undue commotion here today. Or at any time in the past twenty years.

LORD LOVEWORTHY: Not at all, Mrs Monger.

MILLICENT: I am going home now. Miles, I shall expect you to join me shortly. Not because I desire your company, but because someone will have to pick up the bits of furniture and men's undergarments you shall find scattered upon the lawn.

MILES: You don't mean to throw me out of my own house?

MILLICENT: Don't I? Well, I'm sure it shall come about unintentionally as a natural consequence of having all your worldly possessions flung from an upstairs window. Fennimore? Might I borrow your services for the afternoon? I shall be violently redecorating, and your assistance would be smashing.

FENNIMORE: I shall bring a hammer.

EMILY: We will come with you, as well. Won't we, Earl?

EARL: Uh...of course.

(MILLICENT *exits with* FENNIMORE, EMILY *and* EARL.)

LADY LILLIAN: Cyril—

LORD LOVEWORTHY: Yes?

(LADY LILLIAN *cannot find the words.*)

LADY LILLIAN: ...I am quite beyond speech.

LORD LOVEWORTHY: Perhaps a moment of silence, then?

(*They stand in uncomfortable silence.*)

LADY LILLIAN: I shall go to my room now.

LORD LOVEWORTHY: Yes, my dear.

LADY LILLIAN: Alone. (*She exits.*)

MILES: I suspect it will give you great malicious glee to hear me admit that you were right.

LORD LOVEWORTHY: In what respect?

MILES: In light of all that has transpired here today, I do sincerely wish in hindsight that I had simply handed over my bankbook to you at the outset, and spared myself the anguish of having you divulge my sordid secret, slowly and sadistically over the course of an afternoon.

LORD LOVEWORTHY: Well, I am a novelist, after all.

MILES: But now that you have irrevocably revealed that which I'd rather you had not, you will find that your vindictivity has instilled in me such enmity that you shall never see a single pittance of that which you must feel I owe you as a consequence of our wager.

LORD LOVEWORTHY: Oh, but that is not the sordid secret I promised you.

MILES: It isn't?

LORD LOVEWORTHY: Of course not. I'm sure you were already well aware that you had seduced Lady Loveworthy. Revealing so would have served no other purpose than to relieve you of the requisite necessity for discretion in your future indiscretions.

MILES: But what else is there?

LORD LOVEWORTHY: You haven't thought to ask me how I came to discover the affair between my wife and yourself.

MILES: I assume you read it in her diary, as you've already confessed.

LORD LOVEWORTHY: Indeed, I did. I read her diary.

MILES: Just as I thought.

LORD LOVEWORTHY: But such an incursion on privacy seems out of character for me, don't you think?

MILES: So it does. You must have been quite out of your mind with jealousy to have done it.

LORD LOVEWORTHY: Jealousy over what? An affair I knew nothing about? A betrayal I had yet to uncover?

MILES: Well, what then? You are trying the narrow limits of my patience.

LORD LOVEWORTHY: Your patience could use the exercise, as it may soon be the only virtue to which you can lay claim.

MILES: Oh!

LORD LOVEWORTHY: As you know, Miles, I am well-traveled. I like to think that's how my daughter contracted her own incurable wanderlust. When Emily was a child, I often regaled her with exotic tales of primitive civilizations on disease-infested continents I had visited in my youth.

MILES: Yes, in fact, your debut novel was little more than a tedious travelogue of your first trip to France.

LORD LOVEWORTHY: It was on that fateful foray that I incurred a Parisian infection which was to prove my eventual undoing. For it was several years later, in the first year of my marriage, that persistent symptoms forced me to leave my newlywed wife for a week-long sojourn to a certain medical spa in Athens. There, I received a grave and unmentionable diagnosis.

MILES: Say no more.

LORD LOVEWORTHY: Devastated, I returned home to share the unspeakable prognosis with my wife. But she greeted me at the gate with far happier news, for she had become pregnant with our first child.

MILES: You cannot possibly have imagined that I had anything to do with it! You were only gone a week!

LORD LOVEWORTHY: No, of course not. The thought never crossed my mind.

MILES: Oh. That's a relief. Then what was your medical news from Athens?

LORD LOVEWORTHY: That a particularly virulent strain of a disease I had contracted in an ill-fated encounter with a certain French doorknob, had metastasized and

spread to my loins. Left untreated, as any good
physician recommends in cases concerning the loins,
it had ravaged my reproductive system and rendered
me permanently incapable of becoming a progenitor of
anything more palpable than literary works of fiction.
The child Lillian was to bear me could not have been
my own.

MILES: How did she react when you told her?

LORD LOVEWORTHY: She did not, for I had not the heart
to confront her: She was so happy at the presumedly
blessed event. I think she believed the prospect of
raising a family together would mend the offence of
her earlier infidelity. Instead, it thrust the same into
the limelight, by irrefutably confirming that which I
had no cause to suspect: that she had been unfaithful
to me. So I said nothing, and we sat down to tea.

MILES: It is good that you did not act rashly.

LORD LOVEWORTHY: But later that night, I burst into
my wife's room, in a jealous rage!

MILES: Sir Cyril!

LORD LOVEWORTHY: And finding her asleep, and not
wanting to disturb, I stole, instead, her diary, prised
open the lock and read it cover-to-cover.

MILES: Oh!

LORD LOVEWORTHY: When I learned, there, that you
had deceived Lady Lillian, upon first meeting her, with
a false tale of my own purported infidelity, and that she
had succumbed to the seduction of your lies—and a
bottle of cherry mead I thought we were saving for our
wedding anniversary—it was then, and only then that
I realized that, unthinkable as it had seemed, you were
the father of my child.

MILES: But you said I was not the father!

LORD LOVEWORTHY: I said I did not, at the time, suspect
that you were the father. I did not say that I was not
later relieved of my naive credulity.

MILES: Oh. Well...

LORD LOVEWORTHY: Experiencing, in that moment,
the same heartbreak of betrayal and perceived wrong
that must have driven my Lillian into your arms,
I could not bring myself to blame her for what had
happened. Nor could I forgive her. But I had my little
revenge: I published the account of her adulterous
affairs verbatim, under the pseudonym of the lusty
Lady Chelsea of Chatsworth. My vengeance proved a
blessing of sorts as I found the petty behavior, not only
therapeutic, but quite lucrative. Ironic, considering your
ongoing campaign to devastate my literary reputation
had succeeded in rendering my professional career
entirely academic. Yet it was thanks to you that my
pornography has flourished.

MILES: Why did you never tell me that Emily was my
daughter?

LORD LOVEWORTHY: And give you the satisfaction
of joying in the fruits of your transgression? Never.
I kept my secret, and yours, and watched her grow
into the kind of daughter any father, even an impotent,
cuckolded surrogate, could be proud of. And now,
in the wake of her engagement to a noble young
commoner in a dog-skin cap, and on the verge of
their inevitable wedding. I could not be prouder of
my decision to raise her as my own. That is the secret
I believed would convince you to open your bankbook.
That is the secret I thought you would pay any price to
preserve. Am I correct in this? Or have I mistaken you
for a man of any scruples whatsoever?

(MILES *hangs his head in shame.*)

MILES: I will pay for the wedding.

LORD LOVEWORTHY: That won't be necessary.

MILES: What—! But that's what you want! That was our wager! That's why you've put me through this torment. You have won.

LORD LOVEWORTHY: No, I have not. For as you gloated earlier: Our wager was forfeit the moment Emily made her untimely entrance. Your change of heart comes too late for me to profit by the conversion.

MILES: But I am willing to pay you anyway. Out of shame, or guilt, or restitution.

LORD LOVEWORTHY: I told you at the outset that I did not want my daughter's matrimony soiled by unseemly sources. When I invited you here this afternoon, I thought my tawdry second profession was just such a source. But now I see there is nothing so sinful in a bit of ribaldry. Not compared to the moral decay of one such as yourself: A man whose livelihood is consumed with imposing his own ethos on others while practicing none of it himself. I would rather my daughter took up with a saloon-ful of Earls. And had the Star-Spangled Flag of Colonial America tattooed across her bosom, than to see her blissful day sullied with one guilt-ridden guilder from the likes of you. (*He writes* MILES *a cheque.*) I am going to go in now, and see if my wife can ever forgive me for forgiving her in so malicious a manner. When I return, I expect to find you gone. I expect it, because when I return, I shall be armed with a pair of dueling pistols and a family history for slaughtering swine in the parlour. And because I know you to be an abject coward. I expect also, that you will for once show a trace of decency, if only in this: To never set foot in this house, or my daughter's life. Ever again. It is the very least you could do. As a good neighbor.

MILES: I note you make no such stipulation regarding your wife.

LORD LOVEWORTHY: My wife is her own woman, as you know quite biblically, and free to make her own decisions. However, I don't suspect she'll be quite so receptive to your inducements, henceforward. But you are welcome to try. I rather think I shall enjoy the attempts. And the target practice. *(Politely)* Our business being concluded, Mister Monger, I bid you "good day". Leave the key on the table. *(He exits.)*

(MILES hangs his head. Silence. He takes a key out of his pocket, and leaves it on the parlour table, as he exits.)

END OF PLAY